WITHDRAWN

TWO ESSAYS ON ORGAN DESIGN

1. Mount Calvary Church, Baltimore: Andover Organ Company.

TWO ESSAYS
ON
ORGAN DESIGN

I. ORGAN DESIGN AND ORGAN PLAYING

II. REDISCOVERING CLASSIC ORGAN
BUILDING IN AMERICA

BY

JOHN FESPERMAN

RALEIGH

THE SUNBURY PRESS

1975

786,63
F413†
1975

Library of Congress Cataloging in Publication Data

Fesperman, John T.
  Two essays on organ design.

  Includes bibliographies and index.
  CONTENTS: Organ design and organ playing.—Rediscovering classic organ building in America.
  1. Organ—Addresses, essays, lectures. 2. Organ—Construction. 3. Organs—United States. I. Title.
ML550.F43   786.6'3   75-9897
ISBN 0-915548-01-1

LIBRARY OF CONGRESS CATALOG CARD NUMBER: 75-10153

Printed for The Sunbury Press by Bynum Printing Company, Raleigh.

vi

To the Memory of
Frank Bozyan and Melville Smith
Teachers and Friends

vii

CONTENTS

Prologue

Acknowledgments

Plates

ERRATA

page ix, line 28 — For "Electicism" read "Eclecticism".

page xi — The photograph of the Schnitger at Steinkirchen was generously furnished by John Brombaugh.

page 43, line two — Read "builds the 1893 organ by the Johnson Organ Co. in Grace Church, Sandusky, Ohio."

page 82, line two — For "ELECTICISM" read "ECLECTICISM".

page 87, line three — For "Clarion" read "Clairon".

PLATES

ACKNOWLEDGMENTS

Many patient and knowledgeable colleagues have supplied information about instruments and events cited here. Among those to whom gratitude is due for advice, interviews and documents are: Sherodd Albritton, Rudolph von Beckerath, E. Power Biggs, Anthony Bufano, Walter Blodgett, Edward W. Flint, Charles Fisk, D. A. Flentrop, Will Headlee, Chick Holtkamp, Arthur Howes, Lawrence King, Allen B. Kinzey, Noel Mander, Danny Morris, Robert Noehren, Barbara Owen, William Parsons, Arthur Poister, Arthur Quimby, Robert Sipe, Mrs. Melville Smith, and Carl Weinrich.

Special appreciation is due Richard Parsons III who encouraged and supported the author throughout, and to Margaret Epes of the Smithsonian staff and Mary Louise Brandt of the publisher's staff for long-suffering editorial assistance.

The Photographs

2, Peter Heman, Basel; 4, Sydney W. Newbery, London; 10 and 11, Chick Holtkamp; 20, 21, Barbara Owen; 22, Anastasi of Boston; 23, Charles B. Fisk; 1, 5-9, 12, 13, 16-19, 24, Smithsonian photograph.

PROLOGUE

This book is for lovers of music who also are fascinated by that most intricate of all instruments, the organ. It is written with the bias of a performer who believes in the integrity of the instrument as a work of art and as a delicate machine which must work well. Evident throughout is the conviction that the classic principles, observed by organ builders of the seventeenth and eighteenth centuries and implicit in all the repertoire of that period, remain valid today, and that to ignore them is to compromise the identity of the instrument.

Part I deals with the need for the player to understand the nature of the instrument and its repertoire, as developed in Europe up to the early 18th century. Part I characterizes the organ as a musical instrument and defines the principles of classic design. It is, in fact, like a comprehensive introductory organ lesson, which might be given to an unusually perceptive and highly motivated student. Part I seeks to show why it is essential for the musician to understand the organ and its music in terms of its early history.

Part II is a chronological history of the recent past in American organ building. It documents the events which brought classic design principles back to organ building in this country and traces the influences which made possible the building of the first sizable organ designed wholeheartedly in accord with these principles. The organ is the one built in 1961 for Mount Calvary Church, Baltimore. This organ is a true work of art which works well, and is also an inescapably "American" accomplishment that reflects Yankee ingenuity as well as musical and technical skill. The many fine instruments which have appeared in this country since 1961 are not discussed only because of the limited scope of the study, which ends with that year.

The central musical fact, rediscovered between roughly 1930 and 1960, was that the organ could be fully understood only in relation to its repertoire. The renaissance which has taken place is essentially a musical one, and the thread which binds it together is the collaboration between musicians and organ builders. It took both Walter Holtkamp and Melville Smith, for instance, to produce the 1933 Positiv in the Cleveland Museum, and so it went with each breakthrough from Cleveland to Boston to Baltimore.

xiii

PART I

ORGAN DESIGN AND ORGAN PLAYING

I

THE NATURE OF THE ORGAN

Which of us has ever heard talk of art as other than a realm of freedom? This sort of heresy is uniformly widespread because it is imagined that art is outside the bounds of ordinary activity . . . The more constraints one imposes, the more one frees oneself of the chains that shackle the spirit.[1]

A Wind Instrument

The organ is first of all a wind instrument. An understanding of this characteristic is fundamental to any understanding of how the instrument is best played, what musical textures are appropriate to it, and what sorts of sounds may reasonably be expected from it.

Since rhythm in organ playing depends not only on the factors of separation, duration, anticipation and delay but also on the speech of winded pipes, it must be treated as a wind instrument; or there can be no rhythm. Since (unlike other wind instruments) there is no possibility of altering a sound after it has begun, these factors assume even more importance. That its essential nature is often overlooked is unfortunately borne out by the frequency with which one hears virtuosic performances, tolerated only by other organists, which are characterized by unrhythmic articulation and unrealistic *tempi.*

As to pipe speech: a long or low-pitched flue pipe speaks slower than a short or treble pipe; a stopped pipe speaks faster than an

---

[1] Igor Stravinsky in *Poetics of Music.*

open one of the same pitch; a pipe of wide scale speaks quicker than one of narrower scale; a reed pipe may speak more or less promptly than a flue pipe, depending on pitch and quality (as well as style of voicing); a flue pipe with unusually low or unusually high cut-up may either speak slowly or with excessive attack noises.

Articulation and Rhythm

A knowledge of pipe speech is essential to the player because it informs his articulation: the way in which he employs the factors of separation, duration, anticipation, and delay to give life to a melodic line. The importance of rhythmic articulation is most obvious in the case of the Pedal, where low pitches are likely to predominate. For instance, an exaggerated detaché in the low register of the Pedal, especially when using 16' and 8' sound, will not result in clarity, but in lack of proper speech, since a long pipe takes more time to build up to its full speech. If Pedal notes are too short, there may be no sound at all. Similarly, in manuals or pedal, unrelieved detaché playing not only does not produce clarity, it precludes rhythm.

As to accent: Maximum accent is achieved by separating the accented note from its predecessor, lengthening it, and delaying it ever so slightly; consistent detaché articulation, especially in polyphonic textures, makes for confusion and lack of melodic direction.

Finally, no wind instrument is realistically thought of as a "legato" instrument — although one sometimes hears this description used inaccurately of the organ. This description may well derive from the days of electric-action instruments buried in chambers at some distance from the keyboards, but it is quite meaningless when applied to the organ of the 17th or 18th century. It does, however, suggest one expressive aspect of organ technique: it is often possible to alter the speech of the pipes by deft and sensitive depressing and releasing of the keys and by using a firm or gentle force. On a well-regulated action, attack noises can be reduced by a gentle depression of the key and a unique legato achieved; conversely, a crisp depression of the key will produce a crisp attack.

Several Instruments in One

The organ normally consists of several keyboard instruments playable from one keydesk. Each of these organ divisions — Great, Positiv, and Pedal, for instance — has its own action, housing, and, because of differences in disposition and case size, its own individual character. The task of the organist is to use these instruments together, separately, or against each other, as the repertoire demands. Although other instruments (such as the harpsichord) may have two keyboards, only the organ is, in fact, made up of several entities in different locations. The result is a distinctive stereophonic effect, an identifying feature of the instrument, taken into account by all the classic builders and used to advantage by all composers of idiomatic organ music. The stereophonic aspect of the organ's identity became almost entirely lost in the United States by the early twentieth century, not to be regained until the second half of the century, when builders began serious studies of earlier instruments in Europe.

Any obstacle to the sound, such as the lip of an arch in front of the case, or placement to one side will mitigate the free passage of sound. The result is unfocused, diffused, and less clear projection, which confuses articulation and forces the voicer to make the organ louder (with consequent increase of harshness) in order to overcome the obstruction.

The importance of favorable placement for the organ cannot be over-emphasized. A large instrument of the very highest quality can fail, if its sound comes indirectly or if it is forced, although an instrument of modest size, well-located, can more than compensate for its size because of the free and warm quality of its sound.

II

DEFINING THE CLASSIC TRADITION

All of the characteristics which made early organs so satisfying to their contemporaries as well as to twentieth-century musicians combine to produce an orderly unity, leaving no doubt about the artistic identity of the instrument. By hearing, playing, and studying existing instruments which occasioned the repertoire of the seventeenth and eighteenth centuries, it is possible to outline the fundamental components of design which can be termed classic. The following sections discuss briefly the factors essential to the identity of the organ.

Placement

If any factor can be singled out as more important than all others in influencing organ sound, it is how the organ is placed within the space where it is heard. Optimum placement, with the instrument facing its listeners directly, allows the sound to project unforced and unobstructed. The classic solution from the seventeenth and eighteenth centuries is the rear gallery location typical of European churches. Ideally, the organ is near the back wall and stands high, near the ceiling, thus taking advantage of these surfaces for reflection into the area below. Since it is also free-standing, there is substantial sound energy from the vibrating side, back, and top panels of the case.

Encasement and Architectural Form

The first important thing about an organ case is that, like a piano soundboard, it resonates, and therefore both blends and projects the sound, in addition to masking the "natural harshness of raw pipe tone".

The second crucial advantage of a well-designed case is to provide a separate housing for each division, so that each has its own unique character and location. This distinct separateness produces the previously noted stereophonic effect unique to the organ, an effect which is especially noticeable in the large body of music requiring antiphonal effects. The provision of separate cases for each division is another indication of the affinity of an idiomatic repertoire for the instrument. It is not stretching the point to say that much important repertoire cannot be given a proper sound unless the organ is properly encased.

Although case construction varied in different times and places, the function of the case was always more acoustic than decorative. The clearest example of optimum case design can be found in the organs of the north-European builder Arp Schnitger, characterized as follows:

1. Depth is rarely more than 36" even in very large organs. This has the special advantage of allowing all the pipework to speak easily and simultaneously through the front opening, without obstruction or delay.

2. Wood panels are always quite thin (frequently only 3/8"), thus guaranteeing free vibration of the case walls.

3. Cases are open only at the front, so that the case roof acts not only as a reflector but also as a protection against dust.

4. The height of each case is directly related to the basic pitch of each division; for example, 16' for the Pedal, 16' or 8' for the Great, 8' or 4' for the Positiv, etc. The pipes for the basic Principal stop are always displayed in the case front.

Although there were differences in case design, especially in England and France, organs were never built into recessed spaces, but were free-standing, with their own housing. In some Spanish and Italian instruments, cases became rather wide or even rambling, but they were normally shallow. Thus, they still provided reflective areas favorable to the organ's sound.

A clearly discernible architectural form has characterized the organ since its earliest days. The appearance of a given instrument derives directly from its size and resources. Although the case is related to the architecture of the building, it is first of all a part of the organ itself. Its design and construction must be done by the organ builder, not the architect. The visual design of the case is completely dependent upon the technical design of the organ. The acoustical proportions necessary for an 8' Great case and a 4' Positiv

case produce a given visual effect, not *vice versa*. The shape of the
case depends on the placement of the pipes inside and the space
requirements for proper wind supply and chest area; a shallow depth
is essential for proper projection of sound. All these factors combine to give the organ an honest appearance, which consequently
reflects the size and the basic resources housed inside.

In addition to blending and focusing the sound, the case also
forms the basic supporting construction for the main components
(such as windchests and actions). This is another indication of
how case design is integral to the total design of the organ.

A final note about an important decorative and acoustical part
of the case: the pipe shades. Pipe shades of early organs seem to
have the special function of preventing an overemphasis on any
given frequency. The shades function in this way because of their
configuration, which includes curves, openings, angles, and irregular
surfaces. Thus, modern pipe shades should be made in the same
manner and not consist simply of straight, thin pieces of the same
shape, equidistant from each other.

Acoustics

The optimum acoustical environment for an organ is one which
allows a reverberation time of *at least* 2 seconds,[2] with a "line-of-
sight" projection of sound from instrument to hearer. The "line-of-
sight" location (which always obtains when the instrument is properly placed in a rear gallery) is essential because both clarity and
warmth suffer when musical sound is obstructed or heard through a
constricted opening. Reverberation is essential to allow development
of upper partials in the total sound, to avoid harshness and to make
the hearer feel that he is surrounded by sound. Since the audience
or congregation covers part of the floor, which is a critical area for
reflecting sound, allowance must be made for proper reverberation
when a normal number of people is present. Favorable resonance
and reverberation depend upon three factors: structural materials,
shape of enclosed space, and the ratio of cubic volume to audience
area. It is essential to realize that considerably more reverberation is
necessary for organ and choral music than for chamber music or
other kinds of musical sound. This is the "natural" sound of tall,
long, narrow buildings constructed of hard materials.

The churches which house many of Europe's most famous organs
are often enormous and sometimes possess reverberation times of as

---

[2]For these purposes, reverberation time is defined as the elapsed time after
release of a sound until it is no longer audible.

much as five seconds, even when filled with people. An interesting example is the Michaelskerk in Zwolle, where the organ sound is clear and immediate, despite very reverberant acoustics. In other buildings of great size, clarity is sometimes lost if the listener is very far away from the instrument.

More typical, however, are structures of modest size, such as Steinkirchen in Germany; Noordbroek, Holland; Arlesheim Abbey in Switzerland; or Boston's Christ Church (Old North Church). The acoustically critical factors in such buildings may be summarized as follows:

1. *Structural materials:* The buildings are constructed of hard, sound-reflecting materials, mostly masonry, hard plaster, and wood; and there are almost no sound-absorbing surfaces such as drapery or carpeting. All are less live when filled with people, but still retain an effective reverberation period of at least two seconds.

2. *Volume:* Buildings must be large enough to allow organ sound sufficient space to develop fully without seeming overwhelmingly loud. A rough average for minimal enclosed space in which early organs are found is 125,000 cubic feet (the approximate volume for Boston's Old North Church). Adequate size of the enclosed space is absolutely critical to the sound of the organ: no instrument will sound its best in a constricted environment, because there will be distortion of low-frequency sounds due to standing waves.

3. *Shape of enclosed space:* The structural norm is lofty, relatively narrow and usually with a vaulted roof — in other words the ratio of length to width to height ranges from 5:3:2.5 to 6:2:3. The extreme importance of *height* in these structures cannot be overemphasized: modern buildings with low ceilings may save heating and construction costs, but the reduction of volume is often such that there is no measurable reverberation.

Finally, the acoustics of the building are an essential consideration in performing the repertoire. There are many instances which leave no doubt that a given work was intended for performance in a reverberant environment. A particularly convincing example is the *Prelude in E♭ Major* ("St. Anne") of J. S. Bach, a distinguishing feature of which is the low E-flat, surrounded by rests and sounded alone in the Pedal in the opening and concluding sections of the piece (e.g. measures 44-50). The composer's intent is obvious: the low pitch is surrounded by rests to give it time to resonate and be heard without clouding what comes before or after. In a dead acoustical space, the effect is unsatisfactory because the sound dies away immediately, leaving an unrhythmic gap which destroys the continuity of the phrase. Noting a similar situation in Bach's *Toccata in d minor*, E. Power Biggs has observed:[3] ". . . Ample reverberation is part of organ music itself. Many of Bach's organ works are designed actually to exploit reverberation . . . In general, a reverberation time of at least two seconds, and preferably more, is best for the organ and organ music."

Disposition

The crucial facts to be learned from the dispositions of early organs, regardless of national style, are that: 1) the resources of the organ and the requirements of the repertoire are matched; 2) the instrument itself has coherent form. Reciprocally, the composer or performer took for granted an instrument with predictable form and limitations. For the most part, French music was played in Paris and not in Rome or London, and there was small reason to be concerned about an eclectic repertoire, which simply was not available before the days of easy, inexpensive reproduction of printed music.

Although twentieth-century musical horizons are much broader, the central problem remains: The organ must be designed for the music it is to play. Substantial attention is given to present-day designs in Part II, but it can be emphasized here that these solutions rely on earlier organs almost entirely. They do so for an inescapable reason: The form which the organ took in the early eighteenth century is the same form which still identifies it. This is not to say that valid innovations or modifications are impossible, but to confirm that irresponsible or unsympathetic tamperings with a classic entity can quickly blur or obliterate it. As will be seen later, in the recent past, unlimited experimenting often resulted in a mindless eclectic conglomeration which is not appropriate for making music in any style.

Three general principles underlie all classic dispositions, be they North European, French, Spanish, Italian, or English:

1. Provision for a chorus sound on each manual division (and in north Europe, on Pedal also) based on 16', 8', 4', or 2' Principal tone, depending on the size of the organ.

2. Provision for as much variety as the repertoire demands in principal, flute, or reed qualities and pitches, while avoiding pitch duplications of similar qualities within a division.

3. A careful relation between various divisions so that each has its own identity and is, in fact, a separate organ in its own

---

[3]As quoted in Leo L. Beranek, *Music, Acoustics and Architecture* p. 53-4.

right. (Except in France, repertoire normally did not require coupling divisions.)

Old organs were always suited for accompaniment of congregational singing because the requirements for this coincide with demands made by the repertoire. There was, therefore, no distinction between "church" and "concert" instruments — a separation as invalid now as then.

Wind Supply

The first principle governing a good wind supply in early instruments was that it be free and "floating" as well as adequate. This means that one very large reservoir is essential, rather than a series of small ones (which tend to give too hard and unyielding wind resulting in unnecessarily "straight" and sometimes "jittery" tone from the pipes). Modern criticisms often circulated about eighteenth-century "unsteadiness" are demonstrably untrue; instruments still retaining their original winding (even if bellows are electrically moved) remain in use. There is no musical problem when the organ is properly used for its repertoire. While it may be possible to shake the wind on such instruments, this is never apparent in the normal requirements of the repertoire . . . it happens only when unidiomatic use is made of the instrument.

Speaking of the wind supply for the Schnitger organ at Steinkirchen, Charles Fisk observes,[4] "The very variableness of the effect of the wind upon music of diverse kinds suggests the instrument has a temper, that it likes one player but not another, one composer but not another. It seems alive. You even seem to hear it breathing . . . ." Citing the slight fluctuation in wind pressure when a key is depressed or released, opening or closing a valve under a slider channel, Fisk continues: "One's first thought is that these two kinds of pulse, negative and positive, would be detrimental to the making of music. For most of the old music, quite the opposite is true. For example, consider how the pulses contribute to clarity in counterpoint: Assume a five-voice fugue of the classical sort being played on *organo pleno* . . . each time you move the tenor voice . . . there is in the wind a positive pulse followed immediately by a negative pulse, both of which will be manifest as fluctuations in the sustained tones of the other four voices. In this way the sustained voices help to *mark* the comings and goings of an inner part, instead of simply masking it." He continues by pointing out the effect of

---

[4]Charles Fisk, "The Organ's Breath of Life: Some Thoughts about Wind Supply", *The Diapason*, September, 1969.

proper winding on legato playing, on early music which may become dull due to inflexible wind, on ornamentation, on tuning, among other factors. In summary, his point is that a certain "buoyancy" in the wind supply gives both the composer and the player more intimate control over the instrument and is therefore an essential integrating force in producing an artistic instrument: "The organ has to seem to be alive."

In fact, the limitation imposed by such winding turns out to be a musical advantage also because it has a salutary effect on choice of registration. Furthermore, composers were influenced by this limitation and provided for it in both texture and timbre. For instance, in the music of Bach, doubling of pitches might result in lack of clarity or intonation problems; hence the cautions against it.[5] In French music of the same time, coupling (thus doubling pitches) was required for the *Fonds,* but higher pitches were omitted, probably for reasons of intonation; directions for the *Grand Jeu* specified the omission of the *Fourniture* to allow proper winding and intonation for the brilliant reeds and *Tierces.*[6]

An important aside: the appearance since World War II of "Schwimmer" wind regulators in this country and Europe may be a convenience to the organ builder, but not to the music. The use of such crutches not only insures both "nervous" and inflexible winding; it also precludes a satisfactory tremulant. Tremulants on early organs are essential expressive devices, which ought not to be omitted from modern instruments.

Voicing and Scaling

As the discussion of winding indicates, voicing must be considered in relation to it. Inflexible wind makes for inflexible voicing. In addition to a proper wind supply, the following general priniciples characterize voicing of early instruments.

1. A wide variation in loudness among different flue registers does not exist. Each stop is considered in relation to the total sound to achieve a blended ensemble. Most flue registers are much nearer the same intensity than is often the case with modern organs; certainly there was nothing comparable to the twentieth-century Dulciana or Aeoline except in chamber organs intended for small spaces. Intensity and the added advantage of retained clarity result from the combination of ascending pitches, rather than from overpowerful

---

[5]cf. Adlung, *Musica Mechanica Organoedi* (Chapter VIII:232) Berlin, 1768.
[6]cf. LeBegue, Preface to *Premier Livre d'Orgue,* 1676.

single registers. In general, old organs have a full, often brilliant, sound which (especially in French and Spanish instruments) receives added *éclat* when the reeds are used. Unlike stringed and wind instruments of the period, which are somewhat milder than their modern counterparts, organs make a sound which might seem "loud" to modern ears. This quality is due to a favorable acoustical environment and placement as well as to the voicing, with the result that the sound is live and free rather than hard and aggressive.

2. Careful relationship between the rather high cut-up of the pipes and the toe-hole opening is paramount. Toe-holes in old organs are mostly open, but not at the expense of closing to a hair's breadth the windway at the mouth of the pipe. Character in organ sound depends on the windway of the pipe, which, like a singer's throat, must be open. If the cut-up is made too low, due to too much wind from an open toe, then the windway has to be made narrow. This creates a "pinching" of the sound, unnecessary attack noises, and often an exaggerated development of various upper partials at the expense of others essential to optimum sound. In other words, making a law out of the open toe-hole, can produce some inartistic results. Partly closed toe-holes were not unusual in some early instruments, especially in France.

3. Although "nicking" of lower lip and languid, as known in the twentieth century, was not employed, languids were usually not smooth or perfectly sharp. They were either roughly made or "roughed up" in some way to diffuse the windstream as it passed through the mouth of the pipe. Such diffusion is essential to avoid dullness in pipe sound.

As with voicing, scaling of pipework requires that each register be designed in relation to the others with which it may be used in ensemble. The scale for a 4' Principal for example can be decided only in the relation to the scale of the 8' and 2' Principals and the Mixture. While chamber organs might have similar scales, regardless of the space in which the organ is to be used, the acoustical properties and size of the building must always be of prime importance in the scaling of larger instruments. The result is that scales were variable, not fixed — hence the danger in merely copying scales of a given old organ, since the new organ will be placed in an environment quite different from that which occasioned the scaling of the original.

Key and Stop Actions

A responsive mechanical key action and a mechanical stop action were essential components of the design of all early organs. Both these actions have artistic and technical advantages not found in modern electric or electro-pneumatic actions. Their temporary disappearance in the early twentieth century can only be attributed to the loss of any coherent idea of the nature of the instrument itself. As will be seen later, this confusion was compounded by a fascination with the technology of electricity and with bigness.

The main artistic advantage of mechanical key action is that it gives the player more control over the entry of the wind into the pipes than does any other action. It is possible to change the speech of the pipes in a well-regulated action by controlling the force with which the key is depressed. The player has a sense of directly touching the lever which causes the pipe to sound, and he can therefore play more rhythmically. There is also a slight difference in the resistance of the actions for different divisions of the organ, since a 4' Positiv will have slightly smaller and lighter pallets than an 8' Great. Thus, the bigger sound is properly associated with a commensurate tactile difference. A good mechanical action is also faster than any other, since no intermediate mechanism is introduced between the key itself and the valve under the pipe. By the time the key is fully depressed the valve is completely open.

Mechanical action has an additional artistic advantage in that it affects the size and especially the location of each division of the organ. It requires that the organ be placed in one location, just as any other keyboard instrument must be, and that the keyboards be located within or very close to the instrument. This limitation turns out to be a musical advantage, because it demands that the organ be thought of as an entity and that the player be in close contact with the sound-producing parts of the instrument.

The main practical advantages of mechanical action are 1) It lasts much longer than electric action, because it is simply constructed of durable materials; 2) it is easily maintained.

The main artistic advantage of the slider chest action is that there is only one air source for each note, regardless of how many pipes are sounding. One air source results in both a unanimity of attack and a blending of the sound not otherwise obtainable. Mechanically, the slider action is a simple and durable one devoid of problems of deterioration of leather pneumatics and complicated wiring of electric actions. Fortunately modern materials make chests far less susceptible to damage by central heating than chests constructed in the days when dessication due to winter heating was not a problem.

Optimum Size

Although instruments of large proportions existed by the seventeenth century in Europe, instruments of less than 35 registers were much more typical. Any increase in size carries with it considerations for the wind supply and action, and organs were ideally in proportion to the size of the building. For instance, a cathedral might have a 16′ Principal in the Great although a smaller church might not accommodate so large an instrument.

Two important points deserve emphasis with regard to the size of an instrument. First, the temptation to make an organ too large should always be avoided. There are multiplying disadvantages to over-sized instruments, including the following:

a) A redundant and therefore boring disposition can result — with similar registers, even at the same pitch, on various divisions.

b) The instrument can become unwieldy for the player.

c) There are problems of added expense and increased tuning problems.

d) Finally, an instrument which goes beyond three keyboard divisions and Pedal (approximately 40 registers) runs the increasing risk of becoming so eclectic that it loses its integrity. It also becomes hard to control because it is disposed over a larger area, making it difficult for the player to hear directly. A good builder will make each register pull its own weight in ensemble and as a single sound, so that endless "variety" becomes pointless.

Most important, an instrument should be related in size to the space in which it is heard and of which it is an architectural part. For instance, a room of modest proportions might be better served by an instrument of 20 registers and a stopped 16′ Pedal register than by an open Principal 16′.

Second, a mistaken objection to mechanical action organs deserves to be deflated once and for all. This is the argument often advanced not so much against mechanical action as in favor of electric action, which presumes that large instruments can only be controlled by electric action. This is alleged to be due to engineering problems involved with connection between keydesk and windchests, which might cause the action to be too stiff, especially when coupled.

Although coupling is only occasionally musically sensible on a "complete" instrument, it is perfectly possible with a well-regulated action. The superficiality of the argument is best shown up by citing again such instruments as the Schnitger organ of 1723 at Zwolle (63 registers, four keyboards and Pedal, with couplers of three keyboards onto the main division). Not only does this instrument (as restored by Flentrop in 1956) have a very satisfactory action, but also it was apparently especially successful in the eighteenth century. It was of this instrument that Joachim Hess wrote in 1774, singling out the lightness of the action and noting that ". . . with all four keyboards coupled together, it was so easy to play."[7] The engineering problems for large mechanical-action organs are quite surmountable; the point is that excessive size is musically unnecessary.

Keyboard Range

Keyboard ranges vary considerably in early organs. In seventeenth-century French instruments, the *Grand Orgue* might well descend to AA; in English organs, the use of a low GG (often with short octave) was typical, along with a second division which might begin only at tenor c, or even higher. The North Europeans were reasonably agreed on Great C as the beginning pitch for both Pedal and manuals by the end of the seventeenth century, although earlier instruments might have begun with FF. In general, the reason for extended bass ranges was that there was either a minimal Pedal (as in France), or no Pedal stops at all (as in England). The extended bass range is occasionally reflected in the repertoire. For example, the *Organ Mass* of De Grigny calls for an AA in the Pedal, and some English music, including that of John Blow, occasionally specifies GG on the Manual. These pitches usually occur only at such points as a final cadence and they do not prevent performance of the music on an instrument beginning at C. (It is often possible to produce the single low pitch needed by addition of a Pedal 16' register for a final cadence note.)

The most important characteristic of early keyboard ranges is that they generally did not go higher than f''' and often only to c''' or d''' (the Schnitger organ at Zwolle has a keyboard range of 49 notes, C-c''' and a Pedal range of 27 notes C-d'). That these limitations were reflected in the repertoire is well borne out by the music of Bach, all of which is playable within the Zwolle ranges. Builders such as Schnitger employed these ranges not merely to reduce the cost of the organ, however sensible that might be, but because they knew that reed stops and higher mixture pitches were extremely troublesome to voice at pitches above c''', and therefore held to the conservative smaller range.

The 61-note keyboard common in the U. S. (but not Europe) is a twentieth-century phenomenon. The added expense and space required to make modern instruments with a five-octave manual range

---

[7]Hess, J., *Dispositien der merkwaardigste Kerkorgelen.*

and a 32-note Pedal, seen in the light of the above, seem unwarranted. Builders would do well to explain to buyers of new instruments that a manual range of 54 or 56 notes (C-f''' or g''') and a Pedal range of 30 notes (C-f') are appropriate to the repertoire, with the exception of a very small amount of recent and sometimes unidiomatic music. The money saved could be better spent for one or more additional stops in the organ.

There were no standard keyboard or pedal measurements for early instruments, although organs or harpsichords in a given national style had similar octave spans and keyboard dimensions. Pedal keyboards were, of course, flat, and tended to be less recessed under the manuals than in modern instruments. This is noteworthy for the performer, since it significantly affects the kind of articulation he can employ. A short time at an early instrument with a flat pedal keyboard makes it immediately evident that the heel was used far less often than in twentieth century technique, simply because it is often impossible to reach a key with the heel. The musical result is a cleaner, less legato style of playing which is implicit in the music, although often misunderstood when viewed only in terms of modern keyboards.

Modern keyboard measurements and the relation between manuals and pedal can be a deterrent to appropriate articulation simply because they are designed for the comfort of the player rather than in the best interest of the repertoire. Also, shorter manual keys affect articulation in important ways, as do the fingering systems in use before the nineteenth century, a subject often neglected by modern performers. It is fair to say that all of these factors point in the direction of more rhythmic and less bland performance than is normal in modern organ-playing.[8]

The use of short bass octaves on many early keyboards has the interesting effect of making large intervals, such as the tenths which occur in the music of Sweelinck and other seventeenth century composers, easily reachable.

Pitch and Tuning

Pitch varied in early organs, even within the same area or town. For example, the Silbermann organ at Marmoutier (1710-26) is one whole step below A-440, while the organ at Zwolle (1718-21) is one whole step above A-440, probably because of limited ceiling height in the west gallery, which would not allow a 16' pipe of

---

8cf. Powell, Newman W., *Early Keyboard Fingering and Its Effect on Articulation.*

proper length for C.[9] The most likely conjecture is that there was
no "standard" pitch anywhere, and differences in "church" and
"chamber" pitches varied, also.

Tuning practices present a somewhat more confusing picture.
One certainty is that organs were not tuned in equal temperament
before c. 1750. They were tuned in meantone temperaments, including various "elastic" temperaments, often into the nineteenth
century. These tunings, now being used again by modern makers,
have the general effect of sweetening some consonances and making
some dissonances more harsh, depending on which intervals or
tonalities are favored.[10]

Since these qualities have a significant effect on the music itself,
the importance of more than one tuning cannot be overlooked. In
the case of the harpsichord, retuning is relatively simple; critical
notes could be changed even between pieces during a performance.
Altering organ tuning is much more difficult because it involves
multitudes of pipes, some difficult to reach and some of cumbersome
size. Problems of meantone temperaments were sometimes mitigated
by having split keys for such pitches as G-sharp-A-flat and D-sharp-
E-flat, on both organs and harpsichords. This was the case with
Bernard Smith's organ for the Temple Church, London (1684).[11]
Organs, difficult to alter, often retained unequal temperaments well
into the equal-temperament era.

[9]cf. D. A. Flentrop, "Restoration of the Zwolle Organ", *Organ Institute
Quarterly*, VII:2 (Summer, 1957).

[10]cf. A. Mendel, "On Pitches in Use in Bach's Time", *Musical Quarterly*,
XLI:332ff and 466ff.

Mark Lindley, "Mersenne on Keyboard Tuning" and "The Clavier Diversely Tempered". MS, Smithsonian Institution.

W. R. Thomas and J. J. K. Rhodes, "Schlick, Praetorius and the History
of Organ-Pitch." *The Organ Yearbook*, 1971.

[11]cf. Clutton and Niland, *The British Organ*, p. 73.

III

APPROPRIATE AND INAPPROPRIATE USES
OF THE ORGAN

The Classic Repertoire

The organ music of the major composers of the seventeenth and eighteenth centuries constitutes a splendid and unique body of instrumental writing. Although much of it is immediately attractive and "accessible" to the twentieth-century listener, its best rewards come after gaining experience with the various styles employed. For example, an English or French work based on antiphonal effects will immediately charm most hearers, while a chorale-prelude based on an unknown tune or an intricate polyphonic piece may leave them initially unmoved.

"Old" music is important when it uses an expressive medium such as the organ in a distinctive and moving way. To authenticate any art merely because of its age is as mindless as to ignore the ineffable way in which great art of any period communicates to the present day. Equally inadmissible is the championing of what is contemporary, as though it had no origins in history. The reason for performing early music and for providing proper instruments is to allow significant expressions of former times to speak to modern ears in as uninhibited a way as possible.

In the case of the organ, it is no accident that idiomatic writing by exceptional composers coincided with the perfection of the instrument itself and produced music more exciting than before or since. To admire a seventeenth-century Buxtehude or De Grigny is not to diminish the nineteenth century, for both are in fact "old" to listeners in these days, and both require a sympathy, an openness to stylistic languages partly intuitive and partly learned. The intelligent amateur will also find that his earlier acquaintance with nineteenth-century music will be enhanced by his efforts with the earlier repertoire.

Because the medium and the music are inseparable, the point for the player is unmistakable: the repertoire can be best performed with knowledge of the original resources for which it was intended. The examples at the end of Part I can be most profitably considered with actual situations and specific music in mind. Because the requirements of the repertoire are immutably bound to the resources of the instruments themselves, observations for linking the repertoire to appropriate instruments accompany each example.

The Nineteenth Century

A rarely made but fundamental observation about nineteenth-century organ building is that until the time of electric action it had not departed drastically from the principles of the early eighteenth century. Nearly all the repertoire of that century — certainly that of Mendelssohn, Brahms, and Franck — was intended for instruments not radically different from those of more than a century earlier. Even the late nineteenth-century work of Aristide Cavaille-Coll is closer to the eighteenth-century French organ than to most eclectic mid-twentieth-century instruments.

The deluge came at the end of the nineteenth century and in the early years of the twentieth, when it became possible to make instruments so large and so eclectic that composers such as Vierne and Widor began to make demands which were less and less suited to the idiom. When due largely to the introduction of electric action the organ lost its limitations, it also lost its identity.

In the case of the harpsichord, nineteenth-century changes in musical taste led to that instrument's being ignored, rather than to radical changes in the instrument itself. The fate of the organ was more complicated, both because of its institutionalized use in the church and because organs were immovable and expensive. It was in this period that a fascinating but bewildering attempt was made to make the organ perform in a symphonic or orchestral way. So, the confluence of new technology and a new symphonic taste led to a comprehensive, if short-lived, attempt to alter the nature of the instrument. A fuller discussion of how this came about will be found in Part II. "The Demise up to 1930."

A profusion of mechanical devices, which make it possible to change quickly from one sound to another (for instance, an extensive combination action) has little to do with the requirements of the repertoire and is likely to compromise the integrity of the instrument. The relatively minor question of the swell box is often exaggerated in the interest of "flexibility". It is sufficient to note that a swell, provided it opens a full 90 degrees, can be incorporated into an encased organ without destroying the design, however debatable its musical value might be. *The major concern must be lavished on the things that are essential to the success of any design* — placement, acoustics, the shallow case, action — rather than being dissipated in aimless bickering over trifles. Whether an instrument reflects French, German, English, or whatever ideas is far less important than whether it can be well heard by the listener and sensitively controlled by the player.

Such artistic wrong-headedness is often found in organists who have been brought up with electric-action instruments not well-suited to any idiomatic repertoire. Like looking through the wrong end of a telescope, the issue is up-ended by attempts to adapt idiomatic music to inadequate instruments. Seen for what it is, this concern for expressiveness is misguided. It forces into even clearer view the fact that the music itself cannot make sense on an instrument whose design ignores either its repertoire or its inherent form.

The cardinal point for the present-day performer is that nineteenth-century repertoire of genuine musical worth can be adequately performed on an instrument designed in the traditional manner. The notion that this is not possible stems from a misunderstanding of basic design principles common to the organ in any style-period, from unrealistic and unidiomatic requirements sometimes associated with "service-playing", and from completely unmusical and unartistic attitudes about nineteenth-century music. Aside from this, it cannot be helped that a fair amount of dismal music, created for the organ during its period of decline, is hardly worth consideration by serious musicians.

Service and Ensemble Music

That the organ is most successful as a solo instrument is borne out by the fact that only a small percentage of the repertoire involves other instruments. An obvious reason for this is the fixed location of the instrument, which sometimes makes coordination with other instruments difficult. A less obvious reason is the problem of intonation, which arises because the temperament of an organ is difficult to alter. No keyboard instrument, of course, is ever perfectly in tune with a chorus, which can shift into perfect intonation, regardless of the tonality, just as a wind player or violinist can. This tuning problem is even more noticeable with the organ than with other keyboard instruments, due to its sustained sound, which remains at a constant dynamic level. Hence, ensemble music using the organ (of which Bach's *cantatas* or Handel's 22 *concerti* are good examples) generally employs the instrument either for *continuo* (as Handel did in his *tutti* sections) or as a solo voice, as in the *concertino* sections. There are exceptions, of course, but the general practice is clear.

Similarly, the organ is not very satisfactory when used as a part of the orchestra, due to problems of intonation, location of sound source, and to the fact that it tends to be metamphorphosed by similar sound from the wind sections. Even more unsatisfactory, where ensemble intonation is concerned, is the combination of organ and choir, as in "accompanied" anthems, compared to the use of the organ for *continuo* only, avoiding doublings of voice parts.

Some highly questionable compromises in organ design are frequently made, with the justification that the organ must be made to "accompany", to produce sounds and gradual dynamic changes comparable to those of the nineteenth-century orchestra. This is against the nature of the instrument and always results in diminishing its ability to play its own repertoire.

Because trying to use the organ as an orchestra involves compromise from the start, usually without any complete understanding of what is at stake, it also presupposes a variable standard for musical performance in church. This variable standard is singularly critical for organs and organ music, since the organ is used more often in church than elsewhere. This is a painful reminder that the high artistic standards originally associated with organ music and "church" music in general are often hopelessly blurred by inept performances and badly-designed organs. The attitude which allows a different (and lower) standard for music in church than in the real musical world is both recent and specious. It might also be observed that churches get what they deserve, or at least what they pay for, whenever a limp artistic outlook is tolerated.

Treating the organ as an orchestra leads to the unmusical demands often made on it in the interest of "service-playing." Such a use often degenerates into providing background music, a task for which the organ is not well-suited, and which by its very nature demeans both the instrument and the music. The time-honored practice of improvisation is often both appropriate and exciting, but the attempt to create a "mood" conducive to corporate worship through aimless sound effects is suspect because of its implicit sentimentality. It also precludes the integrity appropriate to music-making of a high order.

Such inappropriate uses of the organ are a corollary to the attempt to erect a wall between the "sacred" and the "secular" in art, which would separate "religious" music from other music. Stylistic differences indeed exist, say between plainsong and opera tunes, but not necessarily differences of either quality or sanctity. It was doubtless such thinking that prompted Archibald Davison to characterize "sacred music" as that which has a lily printed on the cover.[12]

Service playing need not make unmusical demands on the organ. An instrument of reasonable size can meet the legitimate musical needs of any liturgical situation: Three keyboards make available to the player three separate sounds of different dynamic levels. A combination action, which implies an electrically assisted stop action, is often thought essential for service-playing. As previously noted, such a convenience all too often has a bad musical result, because it enables the player to shift large blocks of sound in ways that have nothing to do with the repertoire and consequently confuse his idea of how the organ is best used idiomatically. The purpose of the organ is to make music. No element of design (e.g. combinations, a curved pedalboard) which is interposed between the player and his intimate control of the instrument can be tolerated merely because it makes things easier for the player. The secondary purposes of the organ (such as leading singing) will be best served by a design based wholly on musical considerations.

Contrary to assertions often made, a mechanical means of changing registration is more justifiable on a small instrument than on a large one. Limited size is doubtless the reason for the "machine stop" on small English organs, whereby antiphonal effects are possible on one keyboard. It is perfectly possible for a builder to provide one or two adjustable machine pedals without disturbing a mechanical stop action (as has been successfully done at Mt. Calvary Church, Baltimore). Although there may be little historical precedent for such devices, their virtue lies in the fact that they do not affect other aspects of the design, although they make it possible to change from a *tutti* to a different sound, a change which might otherwise be impossible due to limited size. Retaining mechanical control over registers is essential, since an electric stop action is always slower than a mechanical one; is often noisier; and (most detrimental) deprives the player of direct control over the instrument.

Chamber Organs

The term "chamber organ" in this discussion denotes single key-

---

[12]In *Protestant Church Music in America.*

board instruments, often but not always portable, of roughly half-dozen registers. Chamber organs were well-known throughout eighteenth-century Europe although their popularity was greatest in England. They were well-suited for solo and continuo use in *concerti grossi* and similar ensemble music of which the concertos of Handel are the most important examples. For other continuo playing, they could be placed near singers or instrumentalists. Although they were modest instruments, not designed for a wide repertoire, there is a considerable variety of single keyboard music which can be successfully played on them: For example, the *manualiter* chorale variations of Bach, Buxtehude, J. G. Walther, and other north European composers, which do not require Pedal.

Since chamber organs were far more usual in England than elsewhere, an English example by John Snetzler has been chosen for description here. It was for such an instrument that the *concerti* of Handel (and less well-known composers such as William Felton) were intended. Also, much English music of the seventeenth and eighteenth centuries, including the voluntaries of William Boyce, John Stanley, and others, can be played on them. This is possible because the division of the several registers at b/c′ made possible two different sounds at once, one in the treble and one in the bass, and because the existence of a "machine stop" made antiphonal effects possible by instant change from forte to piano.

These instruments were mildly voiced and intended for more or less intimate music. Hence they found their way into private houses as well as into the opera house or theatre. The charm of their sound and, as made by Snetzler, exquisite voicing compensates for their limited function. Certainly, an appropriate performance of a Handel concerto using proper strings and winds and a good chamber organ instantly proclaims the superiority of the original forces over the larger and louder organs and orchestras often erroneously employed today.

The claviorganum, or combination organ and harpsichord, was also likely to have been employed for continuo, since it allowed switching from one instrument to the other as occasion required. Although several claviorgana still exist, and Dom Bédos even gives instructions for making them, their use does not appear to have been very widespread.

IV

EXAMPLES FROM FIVE CLASSIC STYLES
WITH NOTES ON THE REPERTOIRE

The descriptions which follow have been chosen to provide a summary reference for comparing the resources of organs in different styles in order to show how each fits its native repertoire uniquely. Other equally instructive examples could as well have been selected, and alternates will quickly occur to the knowledgeable reader. Two considerations influenced the choices made: first, the need to find a more or less typical example for each style, even though it might not be a particularly famous instrument; second, the need to find instruments which could be photographed and whose facades, at least, remain largely unaltered.

Although the interiors of several of the example instruments may be different from the original dispositions, owing either to a series of "restorations" or to replacement of part or even all of the original pipes and mechanisms, at least the visual forms remain. Insofar as they are known, changes from the original are noted in general and when possible, in detail. With the exception of the Mexico City and St. Paul's Cathedral organs, the other examples have been restored in accord with the plan of one of the major builders who created or revised them before 1760. These instruments still exist to be heard and played and their resources are closely related to a major segment of the repertoire.

The Mexico City instrument, built in Madrid by Don Jorge De Sesma, was chosen both because it serves as an example of the Spanish style and also because it points up the huge treasure of early instruments until recently almost unknown and neglected on the North American continent. It is hoped that a restoration will soon be effected under the auspices of the Mexican Department of Historic Monuments. Finally, an accurate disposition for this, the older of the two Cathedral organs, is here published for the first time; due to the condition of the instrument, earlier descriptions had inevitably contained errors which have been corrected in the course of studies under the auspices of the Smithsonian Institution.[13]

NORTH EUROPE

The Steinkirchen organ is a beautifully proportioned instrument for the north European music of its time: the chorale preludes of Buxtehude or Bach as well as the larger works by such composers are admirably suited to it. It differs most strikingly from French instruments in that the *Pedal* division contains a complete flue chorus as well as a variety of reed stops for use in the *Plenum*, for *cantus* playing or for trio basses. It is also a clear example of the *werk* principle, with the *Pedal* based on a 16′ Principal, the *Hauptwerk* on an 8′ Principal and the *Brustwerk* on a 2′ Principal, each reflected in the height of the case of its division.

Each of the divisions has a complete and independent flue chorus. There are numerous combinations involving mutations or reeds for both solo playing and trio playing, and typically, the divisions are very similar in size. In north European organs, the *Brust* or *Positiv* was intended to be a real equal to the *Hauptwerk*, in contrast to the subsidiary *Petit Jeu* or the *Echo* in French instruments. Finally, the voicing and scaling as well as the disposition of these instruments made them especially well-suited for polyphonic music. This is another reason for the extensive Pedal scheme, which can match the other divisions at a variety of pitches or at the levels of intensity needed for a polyphonic line. A manual to Pedal coupler is therefore not provided because it is not needed.

---

[13]cf. Fesperman, J. and Hinshaw, D., "New Light on North America's Oldest Instruments: Mexico", *Organ Yearbook*, 1972, and Hinshaw, D., "Four Centuries of Mexican Organs", *Music*, May, June, 1969.

THE ARP SCHNITGER ORGAN
Steinkirchen, 1687[14]
Restored by Rudolph von Beckerath, 1955

Hauptwerk
- 16′ Quintadena
- 8′ Principal
- 8′ Rohrflöte
- 4′ Oktave
- 2 2/3′ Nasat
- 2′ Oktave
- 2′ Gemshorn
- 1 1/3′ Mixtur IV-VI
- Cimbel III
- 8′ Trompete
- 2 2/3′ Rauschpfeife II

Brustwerk
- 8′ Gedeckt
- 4′ Rohrflöte
- 1 1/3′ Quinte
- 2′ Oktave
- 2′ Spitzflöte
- Tertian II (1 3/5′ + 1 1/3′)
- 2/3′ Scharf III-IV
- 8′ Krummhorn
- Tremulant

Pedal
- 16′ Principal
- 8′ Oktave
- 4′ Oktave
- 2′ Nachthorn
- 1 1/3′ Mixtur IV-V
- 2 2/3′ Rauschpfeife II
- 16′ Posaune
- 8′ Trompete
- 2′ Kornett

Manual Coupler
Cimbelstern

Von Beckerath notes that the Pedal Mixture was missing and had to be replaced when the organ was restored by him. Also, in 1720 (the same year when the Pedal Mixture was replaced by a Quinte 5 1/3′), the Rauschpfeife on the Hauptwerk and the Quinte 1 1/3′ on the Brustwerk were replaced by a Sesquialtera II and a Quinte 2 2/3′ respectively. These remain in the organ after the restoration.

---

[14]Courtesy of Rudolph von Beckerath.

FRANCE/ALSACE:

THE SILBERMANN ORGAN AT MARMOUTIER ABBEY
1709/1746[15]
André Silbermann, 1709-10, and Jean André Silbermann, 1746

Grand Orgue
- 16' Bourdon
- 8' Montre
- 8' Bourdon
- 4' Prestant
- 2' Doublette
- 2 2/3' Nasard
- 1 3/5' Tierce
- Cornet V (from c')
- Fourniture III
- Cymbale III
- 8' Trompette
- 4' Clarion
- 8' Voix Humaine
- Tremblant

Positiv
- 8' Bourdon
- 4' Prestant
- 2' Doublette
- 2 2/3' Nasard
- 1 3/5' Tierce
- Fourniture III
- 8' Cromorne

Recit
- 8' Bourdon
- 4' Prestant
- Cornet III

Pedalier
- 16' Subbass
- 8' Octave
- 4' Prestant
- 16' Bombarde
- 8' Trompette

In 1955 this instrument was restored to its mid-eighteenth-century state by Muhleisen and Kern. The most important difference between the 1709-10 organ and the 1746 instrument is in the Pedal. The earlier organ had only one 8' (?) register, indicating the Pedal was intended primarily for trio basses, in typical French style.

---

[15]As given by Melville Smith in jacket notes for *A Treasury of Early French Organ Music*, CRM 505, Cambridge Records, Inc.

THE JEAN ANDRE SILBERMANN ORGAN
Arlesheim, Switzerland, 1761[16]

Hauptwerk (C-e''')
- 16' Bourdon
- 8' Montre
- 4' Prestant
- Cornet V (from c')
- 8' Bourdon
- 2 ⅔' Nazard
- 2' Doublette
- 1 ⅗' Tierce
- Fourniture III
- Cymbale II
- 1' Sifflet
- 8' Trompette (divided, treble & bass)
- 8' Voix Humaine

Pedal (C-d')
- 16' Subbass
- 8' Oktavbass
- 8' Trompette

Rückpositiv (C-c''')
- 8' Bourdon
- 4' Prestant
- 4' Flute
- 2 ⅔' Nazard
- 2' Doublette
- 1 ⅗' Tierce
- Fourniture III
- 1 ⅓' Larigot
- 8' Cromorne

Recit/Echo (C-c''')
- 8' Bourdon
- 4' Prestant
- 2 ⅔' Nazard
- 2' Doublette
- 1 ⅗' Tierce (treble only)
- 8' Trompette de recit (treble only)
- 8' Fagottbass (bass only)

When this organ was restored in 1962 by O. Metzler & Söhne, five stops were added to the Pedal, using the disposition of the J. A. Silbermann organ made in 1749 for Temple Neuf, Strasbourg.

---

[16]From Kobel, Heinz, "Die Orgel des Johann Andreas Silbermann von 1761 im Dom zu Arlesheim . . ." in *Katholische Kirchenmusik*, Vol. 2, 1962, Schwyz (Switzerland): E. Eberhard.

In contrast to Gottfried Silbermann, André and Jean André Silbermann, whose instruments are found largely near the eastern French border, were basically French rather than north European organ builders, and the Marmoutier instrument contains the essentials for seventeenth- and eighteenth-century French music. The 1746 enlarging of the organ provided it with a larger Pedal than was normal earlier. It is important to remember that the 16′ registers are not required for the early French repertoire, although useful for other important music. A more usual French *Pédale* of, say 1700, would include flues at 8′ and 4′ pitch and an 8′ Trumpet, the flues intended for trio basses and the Trumpet primarily[17] for plainsong *cantus* playing.

French repertoire, more than any other, makes specific requirements for sounds, which are usually printed in the score as well as discussed at length by the composers in prefaces and treatises. Briefly, the essentials for proper performance of music of Couperin, De Grigny, Le Begue and composers of the later 18th century are these:

1. A *Plein Jeu* on the *Grand Orgue*, consisting of the 16′ Bourdon (or Montre, if there is one) plus 8′, 4′, 2′ and Fourniture (and Cymbale, if one exists); a *Petit Jeu* on the *Positiv* of 8′, 4′, 2′, Fourniture, and/or Cymbale.

2. A *Grand Plein Jeu*, consisting of 16′, 8′, 4′, 2′ flues plus Trompettes 8′ and 4′ and the Tierce, without mixtures.

3. The possibility to play a Cornet against the Cromorne, with an 8′ Pedal bass and often, alternating between this duo and the *Plein Jeu* or *Grand Plein Jeu*.

4. A Trompette of great force in the *Pedal* for playing *cantus* melodies and a Trompette in the *Grand Orgue* for the *Basse de Trompette*.

5. Provision for combining several 8′ and 4′ flue registers for the *Fonds*, either within a single division or if necessary by coupling *Positiv* to *Grand Orgue*.

[17]cf. Douglass, Fenner, *The Language of the Classical French Organ*, especially chapters IV and V. Cf. also the original Pedal disposition for the Silbermann organ at Arlesheim, page 29.

ENGLAND

THE BERNARD SMITH ORGAN
St. Paul's Cathedral, 1695-97[18]

Great (FF-c'''; no low FF#, GG#)

8' ? Open Diapason
8' Open Diapason
8' Stop. Diapason
4' Principall
8' Hol Fleut
2 2/3' Great Twelfth
2' Fifteenth
2 2/3' Small Twelfth
Cornet[19]
Mixture
Sesquialtera[19]
Trumpet

Chayre (FF-c'''; no low FF#, GG#)

8' Quinta Dena Diapason
8' Stop. Diapason
4' Principall
8' Hol Fleut
2 2/3' Great Twelfth
2' Fifteenth
Cimball
8' Voice Humaine
8' Crum Horne

Echo (c-c''')

8' Diapason
4' Principal
4' ? Nason
2' Fifteenth
Cornet
8' Trumpet

Only the case, designed by Sir Christopher Wren, remains of the original organ. The instrument has been moved several times during its long history and completely rebuilt several times. (For a fuller discussion, see Clutton, C., *St. Paul's Cathedral, The Rebuilding of the Organ*, 1973.)

Bernard Smith, a contemporary of both Blow and Purcell, as well as Christopher Wren, solidified his reputation by winning the competition (over his rival Renatus Harris) in 1688 for the construction of an organ in London's Temple Church.

Wren's St. Paul's case design is not necessarily typical of what Smith would have liked. This is the instrument which Wren is said to have referred to as "that damned box of whistles" because Smith wanted to extend the range downward to CC. Wren refused because of the length of the five lowest pipes.

[18]As given by Clutton and Niland, *The British Organ*, p. 74 and confirmed by Noel Mander, who has copies of original church documents.

[19]The usual English terminology is "Cornet" for the treble and "Sesquialtera" (often without a tierce rank) for the bass of the same register.

However, the disposition of this instrument exemplifies the resources appropriate to much English music, especially that of John Blow and Henry Purcell, who produced more important English organ music during the seventeenth century than anyone else. It also is instructive in registering later music such as that of William Boyce or John Stanley. Typical of the requirements of this music are the following, all of which are possible in this instrument:

A full chorus on the Great.

Antiphonal effects for "Double Organ" pieces.

The use of a Trumpet or Cornet for solo passages (or other reed stop, such as the Vox Humana).

A range descending to GG, accommodating occasional needs for pitches below C. The reduced range of the Echo also fits the solo requirements of the repertoire.

The absence of a Pedal division; the Pedal is not called for in English music until the 19th century.

SPAIN/MEXICO:

The special features of Spanish instruments are clearly reflected in their special repertoire. Most impressive, to see as well as to hear, are the brilliant reed voices, mounted *en chamade,* often on a double-fronted case. These are not only employed as solo voices; they dominate the sound of the flues when drawn in ensemble. Their projection in opposite directions from both sides of the case also makes for dazzling antiphonal effects not possible on instruments in other styles.

Spanish instruments often contained only one keyboard, although they might still be of very impressive size, running to 20 or more registers. Of the greatest importance was the inevitable dividing of the keyboard, usually at c'/c#', so that the practice of *medio registro,* or the use of one sound in the treble and a different one in the bass, became a hallmark of the Spanish repertoire. Either the *Trompetas* or the *Cornetas* might be used with accompaniment by the *Flautados* (8' and 4' flues) in either bass or treble, for example.[21]

The Pedal was of minimal importance in Spanish, as in Italian organs: except for an occasional sustained bass note or for special effects in *batalla*-style pieces, it was not required. The profusion of flue and reed voices on the manual(s) made possible a great variety of timbres, with changes normally required only for each section of a work, as in the *tientos* (variations) which were a favorite device of most of the seventeenth- and eighteenth-century composers.

The Mexico City Cathedral organ (located in the *Coro* in typical Spanish style), facing a slightly later instrument of similar proportions, is a spectacular example of the seventeenth-century Spanish style, with all the resources needed for its repertoire. Since Spanish instruments, like those in Italy, changed little during the seventeenth and eighteenth centuries, this organ would be well-suited for the music of Correa de Arauxo and Cabezon as well as later composers such as Cabanilles.

A second example, located in the church of Santa Prisca, Taxco, Mexico, shows a smaller version, which includes the essentials for instruments in the Spanish style. Restoration of this organ, through joint efforts of the Smithsonian Institution and the Mexican Department of Historic Monuments, is underway at the time of this writing (1975); it should be among the first eighteenth-century instruments in Mexico to be heard and used again.

[21]cf. Wyly, James, "La Registrazione della Musica Organistica di Francesco Correa de Arauxo", *L'organo,* Anno. VII:1 (English summary), and Wyly, *The Pre-Romantic Spanish Organ* . . . , Ann Arbor, 1967, University Microfilms, Inc.

THE ORGAN IN THE METROPOLITAN CATHEDRAL
Mexico City, 1688-95[20]

Don Jorge de Sesma, Madrid; Tuburico and Felix Sans, Aragon

The colonial request to the Spanish crown for the organ is dated 1688; it was dedicated at Christmas 1695. The actual builder is Don Jorge de Sesma with the actual erection of the instrument by his nephews, Tiburcio and Felix Sans; the casework was made in Mexico by Juan de Rojas. "Claro" indicates Principal scale, "Nasarda" indicates wide or flute scale. Where register labels are missing, an English description is given.

Manual I

Treble, c#‑d'''	Bass, C‑D‑c'
Lleno V	
Tolosana III	1' Veinte y Docena Clara
4' Octava Nasarda	Lleno III
1 3/5' Diez y Setena Clara	1 1/3' Diez y Novena Clara
2 2/3' Docena Clara	1 3/5' Diez y Setena Clara
8' Violon	4' Octava Nasarda
8' Flautado Mayor	8' Violon
8' Clarin Claro (?)	4' Bajoncillo (?)
Corneta Magna V*	4' Octava Clara*
4' Octava Clara*	2' Quincena Clara*
2' Quincena Clara*	1' Veinte y Docena Clara*
1 1/3' Diez y Novena Clara*	

*The *Cadereta* (a *Rückpositiv*-type case on the gallery rail) pipes actually complete the chorus for Manual I.

Manual II

Treble, c#‑d'''	Bass, C‑D‑c' (Plus ten notes for Pedal Pipes: C, D, E, F‑B)
8' Horizontal reed (bottom row)	
8' Horizontal reed (second row)	8' Bajoncillo (?) (bottom row)
8' Horizontal reed (third row)	2' Clarin en Quincena
4' Horizontal reed (top row)	4' Orlo (?) (top row)
16' Trompa Magna	8' Flautado Major
8' Horizontal reed	16' Flautado
8' Flautado Major	8' Violon
8' Trompa Real	4' Octava Clara
Corneta Magna VII	4' Octava Nasarda

[20]From unpublished information furnished by David W. Hinshaw, August 1973, after a detailed inspection of north organ in the cathedral.

8' Violon
4' Octava Nasarda
2 ⅔' Docena Nasarda**
2 ⅔' Docena Nasarda**
2' Quincena Nasarda
1 ⅗' Diez y Setena Nasarda
1 ⅓' Diez y Novena Nasarda
Corneta en Eco VII
8' Flauta Travesera II
4' Espigueta
Tolosana III
4' Octava Clara
2 ⅔' Docena Clara
2' Quincena Clara
1 ⅓' Diez y Novena Clara
Lleno V
Sobre Simbala III
Simbala II
16' Flautado
8' Flautado Mayor
16' Bajoncillo
8' Obue or Chirimia
8' Clarin Claro

2 ⅔' Docena Clara
2 ⅔' Docena Nasarda
2' Quincena Nasarda
1 ⅗' Diez y Setena Nasarda
4' Espigueta
8' Trompa Real
2' Quincena Clara
1 ⅓' Diez y Novena Clara
2' Espigueta
1' Veinte y Docena Nasarda
1' Veinte y Docena Clara
Lleno V
Simbala III
Sobre Simbala III
8' Flautado Mayor
8' Chirimia
4' Clarin Claro (Obue?)
2' Clarin en Quincena
(Chirimia?)

**The two Docena Nasarda registers are of different scales.

Manual III (Eco)
All pipes contained in box with hinged lid.
Treble only, c'-d'''

8' Violon
16' Chirimia
2 ⅔' Docena Clara

2' Quincena Clara
1 ⅓' Diez y Novena Clara
8' Violines (Trumpet)

Pedal, C-D-E-F-B
16' + 8' Flautados, drawing simultaneously
16', 8', 4' Bajoncillos, drawing simultaneously

Sound effects: Pajaritos (bird calls); Campanas (bells); Cascabeles
(bells or rattles); Tambor and Timbales (usually
for a storm effect, sounding low Pedal pitches simultaneously — most often C and C#.)

The Pedal keys are connected by pull-downs to the extra ten notes
of the bass of Manual II. None of the manual registers are ex-

tended for these notes, and there are only two composite Pedal
registers.

The pitch of this instrument is *circa* A=420. The disposition is
here given in terms of the chest layout, rather than as the knobs
appear at the keydesk.

THE ORGAN IN SANTA PRISCA, TAXCO, GUERRERO
unknown builder, *circa* 1760
Single keyboard C-c'''

Treble (c#'-c''')	*Bass* (C-c')
Timbales (tympani)	Tambores (drum)
Campanitas (bells)	Pajaritos (birds)
8' Clarin Claro*	2' Clarin Quincena*
8' Clarin Campana*	4' Bajoncillo*
16' Trompa Magna*	4' Orlo*
16' Flautado Mayor de 13	8' Flautado Mayor de 13
Abierto	Abierto
8' Flautado Mayor de 6	4' Flautado Mayor de 6
8' Flautado Violon	8' Contra de 13
Tolosana Clara	8' Trompa Nacional
(2 ⅔', 2', 1 ⅗')	2' Quincena Clara
4' Octava Nazarda	1 ⅓' Docena Clara
Corneta de Ecos	1' Veinte y Docena
(8', 4', 2 ⅔', 2',	Llenos de tres Ordenes
1 ⅗')	(⅔', ½', ⅖')
Octava Clara	16' Povera de 26 Grave
(4', 2 ⅔')	
8' Trompeta (in Eco box)	

*Mounted on front façade.

The pitch of this instrument is a few cycles above A=440, assuming
it was not changed by later builders. There were changes in the
organ in 1806 by Jose Antonio Sanchez of Ixmiquilpan and in 1852
by Manuel Suarez. Restoration work now in progress (1975) has
indicated that the instrument was probably moved to Santa Prisca
from some other location; there is a *Cadereta* case, containing a few
pipes in its façade and evidence of both stop action and groovings
for winding pipes. However, no action or chests exist for the *Cadereta* at present. The pipework and disposition as given here are
typical for Spanish/Mexican instruments of the mid-eighteenth
century.

ITALY

THE LORENZO DA PRATO ORGAN
Basilica of San Petronio, Bologna.[22]
Built 1483; Rebuilt 1675

Single Keyboard, original range AA-c''', no low or high B-flat
- 16' Principale
- 8' Ottava
- 4' Decimaquinta
- 2 ⅔' Decimanona
- 2' Vigesimaseconda
- 1 ⅓' Vigesimasesta
- 1' Vigesimanona
- 4' Flauto in decimaquinta

Pedal pull-downs, probably AA to a, without B-flat.

Italian organs of the fifteenth through the eighteenth centuries were almost inevitably of a single keyboard, with a pull-down Pedal with no stops of its own.[23] As the San Petronio disposition indicates, the resources of the organ consisted mainly of a complete principal chorus, available pitch by pitch, with some duplications of pitch of flute quality. Missing from the San Petronio disposition are two items often found in classic Italian instruments and discussed in Constanzo Antegnati's *L'Arte Organica*.[24] They are an adjustable *Tremolo* and a register usually called *Piffaro* or *Voce Umana* (slightly out of tune to produce an undulating effect), and both might have been included in an earlier version of the frequently altered San Petronio organ. A later organ in San Petronio (built 1595 by Malanini and enlarged in 1641 by A. del Corno) did have a *Voce Umana* register.

For the music of Frescobaldi and later composers, such as Zipoli, (since, like Italian harpsichords,[25] organs changed little for over 200 years) very minimal instruction for registration appears, except

[22]From Enrico, Eugene, *The Orchestra at San Petronio in the Baroque Era*, Washington: Smithsonian Institution Press (where the various alterations made in this instrument up to 1675 are also discussed).

[23]cf. Vennum, Thomas, "The Registration of Frescobaldi's Organ Music", *Organ Institute Quarterly*, XI: 1 & 2, 1964, for a full discussion of the resources of Italian instruments.

[24]Reprinted, Mainz, 1958, with preface by Renato Lunelli.

[25]cf. Hubbard, Frank. *Three Centuries of Harpsichord Making*, Cambridge: Harvard University Press, 1965.

in treatises such as Antegnati's. The possibilities and cautions for modern performers include the following:

A *Ripieno* of principal sound (excluding duplicating pitches with flute stops) was available.

The Pedal, probably of 12 or fewer notes and without independent stops, was used only for such purposes as holding a pedal point, and not for independent lines or *cantus* playing.

Although changes in registration were possible and even required, they were not made in the manner possible on an instrument with several keyboards, which could be registered in advance.

CHAMBER ORGAN (ENGLAND)

THE JOHN SNETZLER ORGAN, 1761[26]
Smithsonian Institution, Washington, D. C.

Single Keyboard (GG/B - e′′′, no G-sharp, A-sharp, B, C-sharp)
  8′ Stopped Diapason
  8′ Open Diapason (from c′)
  4′ Flute
  2′ Fifteenth
    Sesquialtera II (bass to b)
    Cornet II (treble from c′)
  Machine stop, silencing 2′ and Sesquialtera-Cornet
  Swell pedal, opening hinged lid behind cornice at top of
    case

The original pitch of this instrument was approximately A=420; it is now tuned at A=440 because metal pipes were trimmed to this pitch before it came into the Smithsonian collection and was restored.

---

[26]cf. Fesperman, John, *A Snetzler Chamber Organ of 1761*, Washington: Smithsonian Institution Press, 1970.

PART II

THREE CRITICAL DECADES

CHRONOLOGY

1933   Walter Holtkamp installs Ruckpositiv, Cleveland Museum. Melville Smith and Arthur Quimby begin performance of complete Bach organ works at Cleveland Museum.

1934   Donald Harrison, collaborating with Carl Weinrich, designs "baroque" organ for chapel of Westminster Choir College.

1935   Contract signed for Aeolian-Skinner organ #940 for Church of the Advent, Boston, designed by Donald Harrison.

1936   Summer, Donald Harrison and Carl Weinrich inspect organs in Europe. December, Harrison plans Aeolian-Skinner #951, "Baroque Organ, Experimental" for Aeolian-Skinner studio.

1937   Aeolian-Skinner #951 installed in Germanic Museum, Harvard University. First broadcasts by E. Powers Biggs from Germanic Museum, sponsored by Coolidge Foundation.

1938   Weinrich records Bach at Westminster Choir College. Biggs makes first recordings at Germanic Museum.

1939   Harrison designs "Praetorius" organ for Westminster Choir College and Weinrich records Bach.

1940   Walter Holtkamp publishes *Present Day Trends in Organ Building*.

1946   First recital by Walter Blodgett on Cleveland Museum organ as completely rebuilt by Walter Holtkamp.

1947   Opening of Organ Institute; inaugural recitals by Carl Weinrich, Arthur Howes, and Ernest White on Methuen Music Hall Organ as rebuilt by Donald Harrison.

Robert Noehren inspects organs in Europe.

1950   Herman Schlicker, collaborating with Robert Noehren, re-
        builds Johnson Organ Co.'s #2893 in Sandusky, Ohio, Grace
        Church.

1951   Noehren records Moreau organ at Gouda, and at Sandusky.

1952   Rieger studio organs installed at School of Music, Univer-
        sity of Michigan and at Rogers Auditorium, Metropolitan
        Museum of Art.

1955   Weinrich records Bach at Skännige.

1956   Biggs visits Zwolle restoration and meets D. A. Flentrop.
        Flentrop addresses national AGO meeting in New York;
        Flentrop's demonstration Positiv thereafter installed at Ober-
        lin Conservatory.

1957   Biggs records at Zwolle.
        Beckerath, collaborating with Noehren, installs organ at
        Trinity Lutheran Church, Cleveland.
        First Flentrop organ at Salem College.
        Schlicker, collaborating with Biggs, rebuilds organ of Old
        North Church, Boston.

1958   Flentrop, collaborating with Biggs, installs new organ at
        Busch-Reisinger Museum, Harvard University.

1960   Melville Smith records de Grigny at Marmoutier.
        Flentrop installs organ at Alabama College.

1961   Beckerath installs organ at Stetson University.
        C. B. Fisk and associates complete organ for Mount Calvary
        Church, Baltimore.

I

INTRODUCTION: THE 1930'S — BEGINNINGS IN CLEVELAND AND BOSTON

In October of 1933, Walter Holtkamp's Positiv division for the organ in the Cleveland Museum of Art was completed. In December of 1936, Donald Harrison was working in Boston at the Aeolian-Skinner Company on plans for "No. 951 - Baroque Organ-Experimental," the organ which later became famous through the weekly Sunday morning broadcast recitals played by E. Power Biggs in the Germanic Museum of Harvard University. These two instruments signalled the beginning of a renaissance in American organ design which produced fundamental changes in the concept of how an organ should sound, what it should look like, and what sort of music it could best play. Not only organists and organ builders but also the public began to take the organ and its repertoire more seriously than before. While Biggs and Carl Weinrich were spurring Harrison's efforts, Holtkamp was being encouraged and advised by Melville Smith. This liaison between players and makers drastically altered the course of American organ design and returned the organ to its rightful role as a serious musical instrument.

II

THE DEMISE (UP TO 1930)

Repertoire

By the time of Holtkamp and Harrison's experiments, most American organ builders and organists had become largely detached from the great repertoire of the seventeenth and eighteenth centuries. Transcriptions and "symphonic" organ music of the nineteenth century ruled the day, as did instruments designed to play this repertoire. The classic principles which gave form and identity to the organs for which Bach or Couperin might have written were all but forgotten. Serious modern composers, especially in the U. S., paid scant attention to these unwieldy instruments, characterized by ponderous sounds and not very convincing imitative orchestral voices. Aside from Ives's *Variations on "America"* one looks in vain for significant organ pieces from major American composers before 1950.

The repertoire for the classic instruments was idiomatic, taking into account the resources of an organ in the French, English, North-European or other legitimate style. The reasons for dwindling interest in the idiomatic repertoire are many and complicated, but the fact remains that the demise of the repertoire parallels the loss of identity which befell the instrument itself.

In the instruments by both Walter Holtkamp and Donald Harrison during the 1930's and '40's, a renewed respect for classic principles was immediately evident. Holtkamp and Harrison attempted to produce in each division an ensemble sound or "Chorus," made up of ascending pitches topped with one or more mixtures. Although the pitches themselves were sometimes provided in organs by other builders, the voicing and scaling were usually so timid that these registers had minimal effect and were metamorphosed by 8′ sound. This lack of ensemble made performance of most of the legitimate repertoire unsatisfactory if not impossible. The performance of polyphonic music on these organs was especially unsatisfactory. A comparison of the dispositions of Harrison's[27] and Holtkamp's[28] instruments with the Cleveland Museum's Ernest Skinner organ of 1922[29] (which had a profusion of orchestral voices, unison registers, borrows, and extensions) gives an idea of the great change in tonal ideas which was beginning.

Although it is not possible to pinpoint exactly when the decline in American organ design began, it was well underway before 1900. It is useful to mention a few pivotal instruments which had great influence during the 1860's and 1870's. These organs combined an ebbing concern for classic principles with a growing interest in size, experiments with actions, and imitative voices. Consequently, there was reduced provision for the traditional repertoire.

Aside from the instrument imported in 1863 for the Boston Music Hall from Walcker in Germany, discussed later in this chapter, two organs made for the Philadelphia Centennial of 1876 are of interest as signs of what was to come. One, made by E. and G. G. Hook, still exists in altered form in St. Joseph's Old Cathedral in Buffalo. The other, by Hilborne Roosevelt, has been lost. The Hook instrument had a Barker lever action, while the Roosevelt instrument had two small electric action divisions, certainly one of the early examples of this innovation soon to mesmerize the organ world. Both of these organs were large by any standard; both had "Solo" Divisions and a substantial number of orchestral registers. Although there was a traditional principal chorus on the Great divisions, there was minimal attempt at ensemble sound on other divisions. In each instance, the case was more a façade than an acoustical housing for the projection of sound. These departures in the 1870's from traditional principles of design with regard to action, disposition, size, and the importance of the case, already show the direction American builders were to take for the next six decades.

Electric Action

Beguiled by the popular taste for the nineteenth-century orchestral repertoire and the early twentieth-century fascination with a new technology which had made possible remote control of the instrument by electric action, organ builders produced larger and larger instruments which were less and less suitable for playing

27cf. p. 58, p. 59, p. 62, p. 64.
28cf. p. 53, p. 55.
29cf. p. 53.

idiomatic repertoire. Arthur Poister, speaking of the early twentieth century, comments,[30]

> . . . *This was a very fertile and prosperous time for the innovator as well as the inventor. It is only natural that the changes in organ construction were so far reaching as to alter the very nature of the instrument . . . . It was during this period that the worth of an article was determined pretty much by a sort of mechanical glamour. Simple products did not entice purchasers nearly as much as cleverly contrived mechanisms which succeeded in accomplishing the unnatural. Somehow, we do not expect to produce an orchestral oboe tone on the piano, neither do we expect the violin to imitate the human voice, but during this period in American organ history, inventors delighted in perfecting good imitations . . . .*

Donald Harrison summed it up by saying,[31] "As a result of its transformation into an imitation symphony orchestra, the organ not only lost its original character but has come to be frowned on by every musician not an organist."

Enormity

Size mesmerized some builders, and organs of gargantuan proportions were created, seemingly in mindless competition. An organ of seven keyboards was constructed for the Atlantic City Auditorium by the Midmer Losh Company, and the six-keyboard instrument in the Philadelphia store of Wanamaker & Co. was proudly identified as the "largest organ in the world." Just what an organ was doing in a department store, few thought to ask. Organ builders seemed to be bearing out Einstein's observation that "perfection of means and confusion of goals is characteristic of our time."

Cinema Organs

During the 1920's a remarkable adaptation of the organ was found in movie theaters, where large instruments were constructed to provide sound effects for silent films. A growing market for such instruments, up to the time of talking pictures, exerted an irresistible influence on the design of organs meant to play the traditional repertoire. Instruments made for churches, colleges, and music

---

[30] From a paper read at a meeting of the AGO at Syracuse University, April 16, 1951.

[31] G. Donald Harrison, describing the Germanic Museum organ (c. 1937), as quoted in *The Contemporary American Organ*, p. 166.

schools, were provided with extraneous imitative voices, at the expense of registers essential for organ music. Although these organs were fascinating and intricate constructions, their tonal resources were far removed from those needed for any music except background for movies. It was hardly possible for the musical public or students of organ playing to hear the legitimate repertoire appropriately played. One of the results of the theatre organ influence was a brief but booming trade in player mechanisms, for which rolls, usually featuring symphonic transcriptions, were prepared, especially for "residence organs", which became fashionable in the homes of the very rich.

Some of the players of these instruments, despite their distance from the traditional repertoire, were nonetheless in the highest tradition of virtuoso popular performers. During the early 1930's such musicians as the irrepressible Fats Waller, who as staff musician for station WLW in Cincinnati played for the legendary "Moon River" program, or Jesse Crawford, at New York's Roxy Theatre, represent a dazzling popular style, now almost totally lost.

Architecture and Acoustics

Preoccupation with technology and bigness produced a mounting disregard for two most important factors which influence the quality of organ sound: the *placement* of the instrument and its *acoustical* environment. Electric action not only changed radically the manner in which wind was admitted to the pipes, but also introduced the possibility of placing the organ itself anywhere in the building, with the keyboards at whatever distance from it.

The fascination with a new technology not only allowed large instruments to be installed in chambers or partially above the ceiling as at Hill Hall, University of North Carolina (or even under the floor, as in Yale's Woolsey Hall), where projection of sound was hopeless, but also removed the organ from consideration as part of the architecture of the room in which it was heard. Not only was the organ looked upon by the architect as a nuisance to be placed "where it would do the least harm architecturally and the least good musically," but also the importance of a live, acoustical environment was ignored in favor of buildings artificially deadened by sound-absorbing materials. The mistaken fear of "echo" in large halls (designed for speech rather than music) thrived on the rush of the acoustical engineers to insure what they regarded as "clarity." So much essential reflective area was removed that the musical result was a hard, dull sound, with consequent need to provide amplification for speech *and* music. The splendid acoustics provided by well-proportioned buildings constructed of natural materials — to be found all over Europe or in American structures such as Boston's Old North Church or Christ Church, New Haven — were temporarily forgotten. Even churches built in the grandest Neo-Gothic style had ceilings covered with absorptive material such as the "Acoustolith" tile developed early in the century by Rafael Guastavino, Jr. and used in such buildings as Riverside, St. Bartholomew's, and St. Thomas' Churches in New York; Columbia, Princeton, and Duke University Chapels; and countless others.

III

EUROPEAN INFLUENCES AND
AMERICAN ACTIVITY

European organ building had succumbed to some of these technological pixilations, but Europe also had many instruments remaining from the seventeenth and eighteenth centuries. By the 1920's the *orgelreform* led by such men as Albert Schweitzer in Alsace and Christhard Mahrenholz in Germany was underway, taking the earlier instruments as models. It is not surprising that American students, arriving in Europe to study music after the First World War, heard and were impressed by the old organs.

During the late 1920's, Lynnwood Farnam, organist at the Church of the Holy Communion in New York and after 1927 at the Curtis Institute, had a strong influence on his students, including Carl Weinrich and Robert Noehren. Farnam had been in Europe[32] and had brought back ideas which doubtless influenced many in the U. S. His playing had already become legendary, as had the great care he took with registration to insure clarity, despite the often unsatisfactory instruments at his disposal. Carl Weinrich comments,[32A]

> He had a selfless devotion to organ-playing, without any trace of showmanship. Everyone was struck by his incredible technic, by the perfection of his playing and his unerring rhythmic sense. He had an uncanny feeling for registration —

---

[32]*The Diapason* for November, 1923 and January, 1924, carried articles by Farnam reporting on his European travels.

cf. Rizzo, Jeanne, "Lynwood Farnam—Master Organist of the Century", *The Diapason*, December 1974.

[32A]From correspondence with Carl Weinrich.

2. The Silbermann Organ at Marmoutier.

3. The Silbermann Organ at Arlesheim.

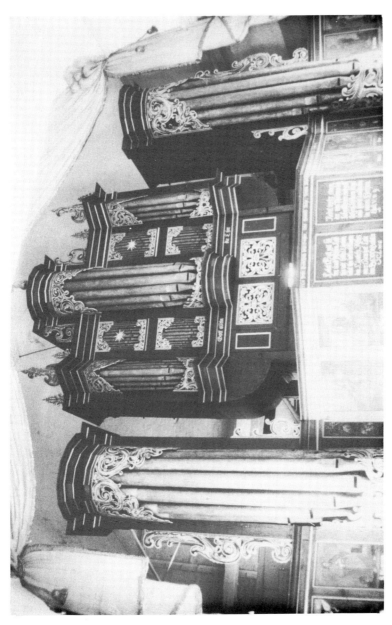

4. The Schnitger Organ at Steinkirchen.

5. The Bernard Smith Organ at St. Paul's Cathedral.

6. The Lorenzo da Prato Organ at San Petronio.

7. The de Sesma Organ in Mexico City.

8. The Organ at Santa Prisca, Taxco.

9. The Snetzler Organ in the Smithsonian Institution.

*he seemed to illumine every piece that he played. There was
nothing of the pedant in his teaching — I think it significant
that his pupils have developed in quite different directions.*
Farnam was destined to be a key figure in the years that followed, but his influence came through his students, because of his un-
timely death in 1930.

Walter Holtkamp and Melville Smith

In 1920 Melville Smith, who had just graduated from Harvard, became the first American pupil of Nadia Boulanger at the
Conservatoire in Paris. He wrote enthusiastically to his friends
Aaron Copland and Virgil Thompson, who arrived in 1921 to become her students.[33] Smith was an organist and in addition to
studying theory and composition he was fascinated by both the
French repertoire and the sounds of the organs.

Smith returned from France in 1924, his ears full of French
organ sounds. After teaching first at the Mannes School in New
York and then at the Eastman School in Rochester, he arrived in
Cleveland in 1931 to join the faculty of Western Reserve University. Rapport quickly developed between Smith; Walter Holtkamp;
and Arthur Quimby, Curator of Music at the Cleveland Museum of
Art. An almost immediate result of this collaboration between players and organ builder was Holtkamp's offer to make a Positiv division, to be added to the E. M. Skinner organ which was then in
the Garden Court of the Museum. The Positiv was first used in
1933. Quimby describes the beginnings as follows:[34]

*The first step was to test the Garden Court in the Museum
for acoustics, what type of tone would sound best, and how
much. Walter brought in sample pipes which we tested until
we arrived at a plan for the Positiv . . . At about the time
of our collaboration — early 1930's — he had gone to Europe and
had got an earful of the old organ sound, which he began to
experiment with . . . Walter then would come up with a
new stop and Mel would criticize it, so together they would
come up with the right result. Mel was a gadfly, and Walter
the willing subject . . .*

*At any rate, the Positiv in the Museum, clearly visible to
all below, was the first example of an open installation in the*

---

[33]From correspondence with Mrs. Melville Smith. The first summer "American School" at Fontainebleau was in 1921, attended by Smith and Copland.
[34]From correspondence with Arthur Quimby.

*country. It was not then a completely satisfactory sound, but
it was a step in the right direction.*

Between October 1933 and March 1934 Smith and Quimby
performed the complete organ works of Bach, using the new Holtkamp Positiv with the then unrevised Skinner organ. André Marchal
appeared for the first time in the United States, playing ten programs of Bach at the Museum. By 1946 Holtkamp had rebuilt the
entire organ. Its influence on students (including the writer) and
players was formidable.

Walter Blodgett, who came to the Cleveland Museum as Curator
of Musical Arts in 1942 and collaborated with Holtkamp in the
rebuilding of the organ, remarks,[35]

> *After knowing intimately great Skinner instruments in Chi-
> cago and other cities, I became an astonished convert to Mr.
> Holtkamp's principles, after being disconcerted as a bright
> young player by his remark that he could not hear the music
> when I played. At last I became more interested in ears than in
> fingers.*

Of the 1946 rebuilding, Blodgett writes,

> *. . . our intention was to revise the organ in terms of the
> classical concept of the organ as it was during the period of its
> great literature. We were limited and influenced by funds avail-
> able. The entire instrument was removed. Some parts were
> abandoned, others were reworked on the voicer's bench into
> totally new speech at the same or different pitches, and con-
> siderable new material was incorporated . . . This was the
> Nation's first substantial instrument in Classic concept . . .*

Blodgett also notes that changes were made in the organ from
time to time "to increase clarity in color and to reduce the decibel
yield" up to 1966, when "more than a dozen stops were replaced,"
this time by Walter Holtkamp, Jr., who had also made other changes
after his father's death in 1962.

In 1940 appeared Holtkamp's *Present Day Trends in Organ
Building,* in which he advocated slider chests and placement of the
organ where it could be heard. Although he made six four-stop porta-

---

[35]From Walter Blodgett, in notes for the inaugural recital on the McMyler
organ, October 25, 1971; Cleveland Museum of Art.

CLEVELAND MUSEUM OF ART[36]
Walter Holtkamp, 1933

Positiv (Added to E. M. Skinner organ of 1922)

8' Bourdon
4' Prestant
2 ⅔' Nazard
2' Doublette
1' Piccolo 1 - 24 notes
1 ⅗' Tierce 25 - 61 notes
1 ⅓' Larigot 1 - 24 notes
4' Flute 24 - 61 notes
Fourniture III

In 1941, the Flute 4' and the Tierce were increased to 61 notes and the Larigot and Piccolo were removed.

CLEVELAND MUSEUM OF ART[37]
Ernest M. Skinner, 1922

Great

16' Bourdon (Ped.)
8' First Diapason
8' Second Diapason
8' Diapason (Sw.)
8' Erzähler
8' Clarabella
8' Gedeckt (Sw.)
8' First Gamba
8' Second Gamba*
8' Voix Céleste (Sw.)
4' Octave
4' Orchestral Flute*
2 ⅔' Quint
2' Fifteenth
Mixture III*
Harmonics IV
8' Tuba
(*Continued on next page*)
*In swell box.

Swell

16' Bourdon
8' Diapason
8' Gedeckt
8' Spitzflute
8' Flute Céleste
8' Gamba
8' Salicional
8' Voix Céleste
8' Echo Dulcet II
4' Octave
4' Flute
2' Flautino
Mixture III
16' Posaune
8' Trumpet
8' Flügel Horn
8' Vox Humana
4' Trumpet
Tremolo

[36]From Blodgett, *op. cit.*
[37]*Ibid.*

(Continued from previous page) Choir

8' Trumpet (Sw.)

8' Harp (Ch.)

8' Chimes*

4' Célesta (Ch.)

    *In swell box.

Pedal

32' Resultant

16' Diapason

16' Bourdon

16' Bourdon (Sw.)

16' Gamba (Ch.)

8' Diapason (ext.)

8' Bourdon (ext.)

8' Bourdon (Sw.)

8' Second Gamba (Gt.)

4' Bourdon (ext.)

16' Trombone

16' Bassoon (Ch.)

8' Trombone (ext.)

Choir

16' Gamba

8' Diapason

8' Kleine Erzähler II

8' Dulciana

8' Concert Flute

4' Flute

2 ⅔' Nazard

2' Piccolo

1 ⅗' Tierce

1 ⅓' Larigot

16' Bassoon

16' English Horn

8' Tuba Mirabilis

8' French Horn

8' Orchestral Oboe

8' Clarinet

8' Harp

4' Célesta

Tremolo

This organ was first installed above the dome of the Rotunda but it was moved to the Garden Court one year later because it could not be heard. It also had a player mechanism for paper rolls, but this went completely unused.

Borrowing of registers between divisions is evident in the Great and especially in the Pedal, which had only three registers of its own.

CLEVELAND MUSEUM OF ART[38]
Walter Holtkamp, 1946

Great
16′ Quintadena
8′ Principal
8′ Gedeckt
8′ Salicional
4′ Octave
4′ Grossoctav
4′ Spitzflöte
2 ⅔′ Quinte
2′ Superoctave
Harmonics IV
Mixture IV
16′ Dulzian
8′ Schalmey

Pedal
32′ Contrabass
16′ Major Bass
16′ Subbass
16′ Lieblich Gedeckt
16′ Quintadena (Gt.)
8′ Octave
8′ Gedeckt
5 ⅓′ Quinte
4′ Choralbass
4′ Nachthorn
3 ⅕′ Tierce
2′ Piccolo
Mixture III
16′ Contra Posaune
16′ Dulzian (Gt.)
8′ Trumpet
8′ Cromorne
4′ Schalmey (Gt.)

Swell
8′ Geigen Principal
8′ Chimney Flute
8′ Quintaton
8′ Gamba
8′ Gamba Céleste
4′ Octave Geigen
4′ Bourdon
2′ Blockflöte
2′ Octavlein
Dolce Cornet III
Plein Jeu V
16′ Contra Fagott
8′ Trompette
4′ Clarion
8′ Vox Humana
Tremolo

Positiv
8′ Copula
4′ Prestant
4′ Rohrflöte
2 ⅔′ Nazard
2′ Doublette
1 ⅗′ Tierce
Fourniture III
8′ Concert Flute
8′ Dulciana
8′ Erzähler Céleste II
4′ Fugara
2′ Flautino
8′ Flügel Horn
Tremolo

[38]From Blodgett, *op. cit.*

tives with mechanical action during the 1930's, Holtkamp did not venture further in this direction, and he was reluctant to encase his organs. Nonetheless, his artistic integrity and singleness of purpose were major and provocative influences on both organists and apprentices, of whom Charles Fisk was one in 1954 and 1955. Partly because of his rapport not only with Melville Smith but also with other players and teachers, notably Arthur Poister at Syracuse University and Frank Bozyan at Yale, Holtkamp's work was probably more influential than that of any other organ builder in the years just after World War II. Syracuse acquired its first large Holtkamp instrument in 1950 and by 1952, Yale's Battell Chapel had one also.

Holtkamp's influence was also felt by some seminary music programs. Holtkamp instruments were installed at General Theological Seminary in New York and at the Episcopal Theological School in Cambridge before 1960.

Donald Harrison, E. Power Biggs, and Carl Weinrich

If Holtkamp's 1933 Cleveland Positiv was the beginning of the renaissance, it was quickly followed by G. Donald Harrison's experiments at the Aeolian-Skinner Company in Boston. An early collaboration was between Harrison and Carl Weinrich at Princeton, who comments: [39]

> In 1933, when I was appointed to head the Organ Department at the Westminster Choir School in its new home in Princeton, my first task was to design an organ for the chapel. . . . The Westminster organ, built by Aeolian-Skinner, dedicated in 1934, had a complete flue-chorus on each manual and pedal, and was probably the first in which the conventional Choir division became a straightforward Positiv.
>
> In the summer of 1936, Donald Harrison of the Aeolian-Skinner Organ Co. and I went to Germany to hear some of the Schnitgers and Silbermanns. Senator Richards had already written glowing reports of these instruments, but I think we were the first builder and organist to make the pilgrimage! . . .
>
> Donald Harrison's interest in what he saw in Europe led to the construction of two organs, one in the Germanic Museum in Cambridge, and another, the so-called "Praetorius" organ at the Westminster Choir School . . . .

In December 1936 Harrison, who had come to this country from England in the early 1930's, was at work on his firm's Organ No. 951 for which the plans were labelled "Baroque Organ — Ex-

---

[39]From correspondence with Carl Weinrich.

CROUSE AUDITORIUM, SYRACUSE UNIVERSITY[40]
Walter Holtkamp, 1950

Great
16' Quintadena
8' Principal
8' Gedackt
8' Gemshorn
4' Gross Octav
4' Octave
4' Spitzflöte
2 ⅔' Quinte
2' Superoctave
1 ⅓' Mixture IV
½' Scharf III
16' Dulzian
8' Schalmey
Chimes

Pedal
32' Grand Bourdon (ext.)
16' Principal
16' Subbass
16' Gamba
16' Quintadena (Gt.)
16' Lieblich Gedeckt (Sw.)
8' Octave
8' Violon
8' Stille Gedeckt
5 ⅓' Quinte
4' Choralbass
4' Hohlflöte
2' Piccolo
2 ⅔' Rauschquinte II
2' Mixture III
16' Posaune
16' Dulzian (Gt.)
8' Trumpet
4' Rohr Schalmey
2' Rohr Schalmey (ext.)

Swell
16' Lieblich Gedeckt
8' Geigen Principal
8' Rohrflöte
8' Gamba
8' Gamba Celeste
8' Flauto Dolce
8' Flute Celeste
4' Octave Geigen
4' Bourdon
2' Flautino
1 ⅓' Larigot
Sesquialtera II
2' Plein Jeu V
16' Bassoon
8' Trompette
8' Oboe
4' Clarion

Positiv
8' Copula
8' Quintadena
4' Principal
4' Rohrflöte
2 ⅔' Nazard
2' Doublette
2' Nachthorn
1 ⅗' Tierce
1' Sifflöte
1' Cymbal III
8' Cromorne

This instrument has 32 combination pistons and 13 couplers.

---

[40]Courtesy of Will Headlee. Five registers were retained, revoiced, from the Roosevelt organ, no. 423 of 1889, which the new organ replaced in Crouse Auditorium, and two from the Aeolian organ of 1929 in Hendricks Chapel at the University. (Mixture pitches refer to lowest rank at low C.)

WESTMINSTER CHOIR COLLEGE CHAPEL[41]
Princeton, N. J.
Donald Harrison, Aeolian-Skinner Organ Co., 1934

Great

- 8′ Diapason
- 8′ Flute Harmonique
- 8′ Gemshorn
- 4′ Octave
- 2 ⅔′ Twelfth
- 2′ Fifteenth
- Fourniture IV
- Cymbale II

Pedal

- 16′ Contrabass
- 16′ Bourdon
- 16′ Gemshorn
- 8′ Principal
- 8′ Flute Conique
- 8′ Gemshorn
- 4′ Flute
- 4′ Gemshorn
- Mixture III
- 16′ Bombarde
- 8′ Trumpet
- 4′ Clarion

Swell

- 8′ Geigen
- 8′ Salicional
- 8′ Voix Celeste
- 8′ Unda Maris
- 8′ Rohrflöte
- 4′ Octave
- 4′ Flute Triangulaire
- 2′ Octavin
- 1 ⅓′ Larigot
- Plein Jeu V
- 16′ Bombarde
- 8′ Trumpet
- 4′ Clarion

Choir

- 16′ Gemshorn
- 8′ Gemshorn
- 8′ Gedackt
- 4′ Principal
- 4′ Flute d'Amour
- 2 ⅔′ Nazard
- 2′ Octave
- 1 ⅗′ Tierce
- Scharf III
- 8′ Vox Humana

---

[41]Courtesy of Carl Weinrich.

WESTMINSTER CHOIR COLLEGE
"PRAETORIUS ORGAN"[42]
Donald Harrison, Aeolian-Skinner Organ Co., 1939

Hauptwerk
8′ Gedackt
4′ Spitzflöte
2′ Principal
Scharf III
8′ Krummhorn

Positiv
8′ Quintadena
4′ Rohrflöte
2′ Nachthorn
1′ Sifflöte
2 ⅔′ Nasat
1 ⅗′ Terz

Pedal
16′ Bourdon
8′ Gedacktpommer
4′ Koppelflöte
8′ Krummhorn
4′ Krummhorn

[42]Courtesy of Carl Weinrich.

perimental.[43] The instrument was intended for a studio at the
workshop, but not for long. As with Smith and Holtkamp in Cleveland, a fortuitous collaboration arose between Harrison and E.
Power Biggs, himself not long in the U. S. from England. Biggs,
who taught at the Longy School in Cambridge and had been
organist of Christ Church, Cambridge, persuaded Harrison and Dr.
Charles Kuhn, Curator of the Germanic Museum at Harvard, that
the instrument would sound far better in the lofty Romanesque
Hall of the Museum. It was placed in the gallery, its exposed pipes
protected from the curious by an unsightly wire fence. Biggs gives
its early history and that of the broadcasts which made it famous:[44]

> The classic organ in the Germanic Museum of Harvard
> University . . . which is now just a pile of burnt wood and
> melted metal, was really in the beginning just a lucky accident.
> The organ referred to is not, of course, the present Flentrop,
> but the previous instrument by G. Donald Harrison of Aeolian-
> Skinner . . . Harrison had been to Europe and had listened
> to a lot of famous European organs. He had come back with a
> number of ideas which he wanted to put into practice. In those
> years, business was rather slack for the Aeolian-Skinner Com-
> pany, and Harrison proposed to use some of the free time to
> plan and build a small organ to be used as a demonstration
> model . . . The Romanesque Hall of the Germanic Museum
> is a wonderful place for an organ . . . Various people, in-
> cluding King Covell and Ed Gammons had previously observed
> that an organ would sound extremely well there . . . I can't
> quite explain how I happened to be walking around the Mu-
> seum, snapping my fingers and thinking the same thoughts
> . . . I took the rather large liberty of suggesting the idea of an
> organ to Dr. Charles Kuhn, Curator of the Museum. He was
> very sympathetic, but, of course, remarked that there was no
> money available . . . It was really the most fortunate coinci-
> dence of several factors . . . that I was able to suggest to
> Donald Harrison . . . 'why not put that organ into the Ger-
> manic Museum . . . on loan' . . . The organ was put in in
> 1937. Windchests and pipes, I understand, were largely made
> out of odds and ends lying around the factory . . . the console
> was from an ancient Aeolian player organ . . . It sounded ex-
> traordinarily well . . . Of course, the bland voicing did not give
> the organ any articulation and the electric action would have

[43]From documents supplied by the Aeolian-Skinner Company.
[44]From a tape made by E. Power Biggs for the Smithsonian Institution, January, 1973.

precluded the control of chiff, had there been any chiff . . . It took a little while for the lessons, both positive and negative, taught by the organ to be learned . . . I was fortunate to give a number of concerts on the organ, including the Bach organ works . . . James Fassett, Music Director of the Columbia Broadcasting system . . . became interested in some broadcasts . . . with the general interest and support of Elizabeth Sprague Coolidge, we started on a series of ten programs . . . the first one was in September, 1942 . . . the broadcasts continued . . . until 1958 in September . . . all broadcasts were live . . . the announcer leaning on the console with the script . . . Broadcasts continued steadily . . . into the '50's, but in 1954, our ears became stretched, to use Charles Ives' phrase. I had the privilege of going to Europe . . . playing the great historic organs of Europe had for me the impact of a revelation . . . The sound of these instruments was so enormously different and superior. Many things thus suddenly came into focus: the importance of tracker action, of articulate voicing, of the organ case, of the windchest and so on — and particularly interaction of playing action and pipe sound . . . one suddenly realized the truth and enormous vitality of all that Schweitzer had written about many years before . . . but the truth doesn't percolate until you hear, and preferably play, these older organs . . . by the fortunate fact that we were able to bring back from the 1954 tour on tape . . . these sounds, they could be fixed for rehearing and re-examination . . . another trip made it imperative that we should have another sort of organ for the Germanic Museum . . . A new organ was therefore planned to be built by D. A. Flentrop of Zaandam, Holland . . . installed in the summer of 1958 . . . Ironically, soon after the Flentrop organ arrived, the radio programs were terminated. TV was pushing the network radio off the map . . . practically all creative, that is live music, was dropped . . . but as one avenue closed, another opened up, namely more and more LP records . . . In its new home at Boston University . . . the Aeolian-Skinner organ came to a sad end . . . in the spring of 1971, it was the victim of arson . . . Let's hope it can be rejuvenated and placed once again in a favorable acoustical environment. It lived its life, 1937 to 1971, in a period in which it was possible for its useful influence to be the greatest . . . I am enormously grateful to G. Donald Harrison, to Dr. Charles Kuhn, to James Fassett, and to others, for all the wonderful opportunity that the instrument represented.

The regular Sunday morning broadcasts by Biggs and the

THE GERMANIC MUSEUM, HARVARD UNIVERSITY
designed by G. Donald Harrison, 9 December 1936
Transcribed from Harrison's original worksheets for Aeolian-Skinner.

Hauptwerke 2 ½" wind
- 8' Quintade
- 8' Montre
- 8' Spitzflöte
- 4' Principal
- 4' Rohrflöte
- 2 ⅔' Quinte
- 2' Super Octave
- 1 ⅓' Fourniture IV

Positiv 2 ½" wind
- 8' Koppel Flöte
- 4' Nachthorn
- 2 ⅔' Nasat
- 2' Blockflöte
- 1 ⅗' Terz
- 1' Sifflöte
- ½' Zimbel III
- 8' Krummhorn

Pedal 3" wind
- 16' Bourdon
- 16' Quintaton (Hptwke.)
- 8' Gedackt Pommer
- 8' Spitzprincipal
- 4' Nachthorn
- 2' Blockflöte
- 4' Fourniture III
- 16' Posaune (32 pipes)
- 8' Trompete (12 pipes)
- 4' Krummhorn (Positiv)

Positiv to Pedal
Hauptwerke to Pedal
Positiv to Hauptwerke
Positiv to Hauptwerke 16'

BUSCH-REISINGER MUSEUM, HARVARD UNIVERSITY[45]
D. A. Flentrop, 1958

Hoofdwerk
- 8' Prestant
- 8' Roerfluit
- 4' Octaaf
- 4' Speelfluit
- 2 ⅔' Nasard
- 2' Vlakfluit
- 1 ⅗' Terts
- Mixtuur IV

Borstwerk
- 8' Zingend Gedekt
- 4' Koppelfluit
- 2' Prestant
- 1' Sifflet
- 8' Rankett

Rugpositief
- 8' Holpijp
- 4' Prestant
- 4' Roerfluit
- 2' Gemshoorn
- 1 ⅓' Quint
- Mixtuur II
- 8' Krumhoorn

Pedaal
- 16' Bourdon
- 8' Prestant
- 8' Gedekt
- 4' Fluit
- Mixtuur III
- 16' Fagot
- 8' Trompet

Couplers: Hoofdwerk-Pedaal
Rugpositief-Pedaal
Borstwerk-Pedaal
Rugpositief-Hoofdwerk
Borstwerk-Hoofdwerk

The 8' Rankett of the *Borstwerk* may be removed and replaced by a 2' Trompet (especially useful when coupled to the *Pedaal* for *cantus* playing) or by an 8' Dulciaan. The 2' Vlakfluit of the *Hoofdwerk* may be replaced by a 2' Principal. These pipes are kept near the organ, stored in special pipe boxes. Mr. Biggs notes Walter Holtkamp's reaction: "On hearing of these 'convertible' stops, Holtkamp (senior) said 'better keep this quiet, or every organist will want a batch of convertibles.'"

[45]Courtesy of E. Power Biggs.

CHURCH OF THE ADVENT, BOSTON[46]
G. Donald Harrison, Aeolian-Skinner Organ Co., 1935

Great
- 16′ Diapason
- 8′ Principal
- 8′ Diapason
- 8′ Flute Harmonique
- 5 ⅓′ Grosse Quinte
- 4′ Octave
- 4′ Principal
- 2 ⅔′ Quinte
- 2′ Super Octave
- Sesquialtera IV-V
- Fourniture IV (12-15-19-22)
- Cymbel III (22-26-29)

Choir
- 8′ Viola
- 8′ Orchestral Flute
- 8′ Dolcan
- 8′ Dolcan Celeste
- 4′ Zauber Flöte
- 8′ Clarinet
- 8′ Trumpet (unenclosed)
- Tremolo

Ruck-Positiv (Playable from Choir or Great)
- 8′ Rohrflöte
- 4′ Principal
- 4′ Koppel Flöte
- 2 ⅔′ Nazard
- 2′ Blockflöte
- 1 ⅗′ Tierce
- 1′ Sifflöte
- Scharf IV (19-22-26-29)

This organ had "tracker touch", 21 couplers, and approximately 50 combination pistons and other controls.

Pedal
- 32′ Sub Bass (Resultant below low F)
- 16′ Principal
- 16′ Contre Basse
- 16′ Bourdon
- 16′ Lieblich Gedeckt (Sw.)
- 8′ Principal
- 8′ Flute Ouverte
- 8′ Still Gedeckt (Sw.)
- 5 ⅓′ Quinte
- 4′ Principal
- 4′ Flute Harmonique
- Mixture III (17-19-22)
- Fourniture II (26-29)
- 16′ Bombarde
- 8′ Trompette
- 4′ Clairon

Swell
- 16′ Lieblich Gedeckt
- 8′ Geigen
- 8′ Stopped Diapason
- 8′ Viole de Gambe
- 8′ Viole Celeste
- 8′ Echo Salicional
- 4′ Octave Geigen
- 4′ Flauto Traverso
- 4′ Fugara
- 2′ Fifteenth
- Grave Mixture III (12-15-19)
- Plein Jeu III (22-26-29)
- 16′ Bombarde
- 8′ Trompette I
- 8′ Trompette II
- 4′ Clairon
- 8′ Vox Humana
- Tremolo

---

[46]From Harrison's original worksheets for organ no. 940, dated Oct. 25, 1935.

recordings made on the first Germanic Museum organ introduced many students to the repertoire of the seventeenth and eighteenth centuries and also had great influence on the listening public, by exposing them to both the music and the sounds appropriate to an instrument designed in the classic manner.

Other Harrison instruments also had wide influence during the 1930's and 1940's. Among the most important were those at the Church of the Advent, Boston, 1935 (see p. 64); All Saints' Church, Worcester, 1933 (changes by Harrison in 1940-41); and St. Paul's Chapel, Columbia University, 1938.

Recordings and Broadcasts, 1937-1958

Charles Fisk speaks of[47] ". . . the *crucial* influence of the European phonograph records, by which we found out how a classic organ sounded," and continues to say, "None of my early work would have been possible without records." Not only the early 78 rpm discs by Schweitzer and others had influence, but also those made by Americans who were drawn to the European sounds. Carl Weinrich's earlier Musicraft discs, made on two of Donald Harrison's instruments, brought important repertoire to the fore, and attracted wide attention from both press and public. Weinrich comments on his first records made at Westminster Choir College:[48]

The records which I made on this instrument for Musicraft (Westminster Choir School Chapel Organ) brought it a wide audience. In this day, when Baroque music is so well represented in record catalogs, it is hard to imagine a time when this was not so. The Musicraft people broke new ground with their recordings of harpsichord, organ, guitar, voice, and chorus, with such artists as Kirkpatrick, Segovia, Boatwright, Boepple and Mendel. At that time the only available organ records of Baroque music on Baroque or baroque-type organs were two Bach albums by Albert Schweitzer, and a four-record set by four French organists . . . the sound of the Westminster organ, quite unlike what people had usually associated with organ, created something of a sensation.

. . . organ recording has come of age . . . Now this month sees the release not only of the second volume of Dr. Schweitzer's Bach series, but the first important organ recordings to be made by American engineers, two of the Bach trio sonatas,

---

[47]From correspondence with Charles Fisk.
[48]From correspondence with Carl Weinrich.

played by Carl Weinrich on the Aeolian-Skinner organ at the Westminster Choir School in Princeton, New Jersey.

So wrote Phillip Miller in *The American Music Lover* for December 1937. *The Steinway Record Review* for November 1939 reviewed ecstatically not only Weinrich's Bach playing, but also the new "Praetorius" organ at the Westminster Choir School:

> *In addition to capturing the tone qualities of the type of organ for which Bach and his contemporaries wrote, this remarkable organ is also extraordinarily well adapted to recording, and we hear none of the blurred and muddied colors so painfully familiar in most organ performances and recordings of recent years . . . .*

In 1938 Biggs recorded at the Germanic Museum for RCA Victor. The recordings included works of Bach and d'Aquin, and with the Fiedler Sinfonietta, concertos of Handel, Corelli, and Felton. There were subsequent RCA releases, recorded at Memorial Church at Harvard (Harrison-Aeolian-Skinner organ) and at the Germanic Museum. The first Columbia recordings by Biggs were done on the Harrison organ at Columbia University Chapel in 1948-49, and at Symphony Hall, Boston, in 1950. Robert Noehren was recording the Moreau organ at Gouda in 1951 for Allegro Records, and the rebuilt organ at Sandusky, Ohio, about the same time. Biggs' first European album (Columbia Records) appeared in late 1954.

The Methuen Music Hall Organ and
The Organ Institute Quarterly, 1947.

The establishment of the Organ Institute by Arthur Howes and others in 1947 drew many aspiring young players and their teachers to Methuen for summer sessions and provided a stage for some of the best performers from the United States and Europe. Their writings, together with those of European builders and theorists, appeared in the pages of the *Organ Institute Quarterly* during the '50's and early '60's. The most important influence, of course, was the organ in the Music Hall at Methuen, newly rebuilt by G. Donald Harrison with the collaboration of Arthur Howes, Carl Weinrich, Ernest White, and others.

The original organ of 84 stops, made by the German firm of Walcker of Ludwigsburg for the Boston Music Hall, was opened to great acclaim in 1863. It retained a substantially greater number of classic features than the Centennial organs of 1876 mentioned earlier. Of the Walcker organ *Dwight's Musical Journal* wrote, "It

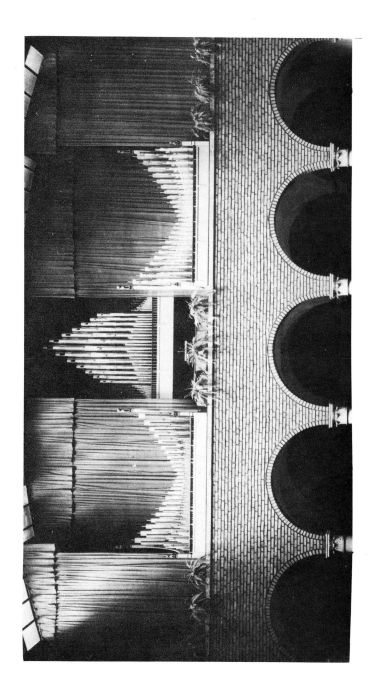

10. Cleveland Museum of Art: Holtkamp Organ.

11. Walter Holtkamp.

12. Melville Smith.

13. Carl Weinrich.

14. E. Power Biggs, Donald Harrison, and Albert Schweitzer at the Germanic Museum.

HAUPTWERKE 2 1/2"

- 16' Quintade (tenor C) as #936 Ch Quintaton
- 8' Principal #45 1/4 spotted 1/2 17th note long flats
- 8' Spitzflöte Com Flauto Dolce
- 4' Principal #57 1/4 spotted 1/2 17th note long flats
- 4' Rohrflöte Com metal Std. Diap. 1/4 mouth spotted. 2 ...
- 2 2/3' Quinte #66 1/2 18th note 1/4 spotted
- 2' Super Octave #69 1/2 18th "   "   "
- 1 1/3' Fourniture IV Pure tin 1/4 mouths 1/2 18th note all #45 @ 8' CC

	CC to F	19 - 22 - 26 - 29	18 notes
	Tenor F# to D	15 - 19 - 22 - 26	9 "
	D# to D	12 - 15 - 19 - 22	12 "
	D# to A	8 - 12 - 15 - 19	7 "
	A# to top C	1 - 8 - 12 - 15	15
			61 "

POSITIV 2 1.2" wind

- 8' Koppel Flöte 4' G up com as 948 tin   4' G to F# to have scales of
  4' G to 2' C but cone at top closed by cap.
  Lower 12 com #2 wood Std. bass.
- 4' Nachthorn - as Wellesley Gt 4' Flute tin 1/4 mouth
- 2 2/3' Nasat - as 948
- 2' Blockflöte - as 948
- 1 3/5' Terz - as 948
- 1' Sifflöte - as 948 tin
- 1/2' Zimbel III as 948 tin
- 8' Krumhorn - as 949.

PEDAL 3" wind

16' Bourdon (stock pipes)
16' QUINTATON (GR)
Ph ⟶ 8' Gedackt Pommer   lower 12 zinc 4' C up spotted
                    scale 8' CC - #56 1/4 4' C up Metal
                    Std. Diap. with solid canisters no chimneys
        SPITZ PRINCIPAL
Ph ⟶ 8' Principal - #45 1/4

⟶ 4' Nachthorn - as Wellesley Gt 4' Flute

Ph ⟶ 2' Blockflöte - same as on Positiv
                    4' - 2 2/3' - 2'
Br ⟶ 4' Fourniture   15 - 19 - 22   all 45 @ 8' CC 1/4 mouth
                                        1/2 17th no breaks

⟶ 16' Posaune - 32 Pipes)
) old Westminster Choir School Swell 16' reed
⟶ 8' Trumpette - 12 "   )
                      A
⟶ 4' Krumhorn (Positiv)

⟶ CONSOLE MODEL A in Studio

COUPLERS⟶ Positiv to Pedal
        ⟶ Hauptwerke to Pedal
        ⟶ Positiv to Hauptwerke
        ⟶   "   "   "   16'

⟶ ALL AS ORIGINALLY LAID OUT

15. and 16. Donald Harrison's Worksheets for the Germanic
Museum.

17. The Germanic Museum, Harvard University: Aeolian-Skinner Organ.

18. E. Power Biggs at the keydesk of the Germanic Museum Organ.

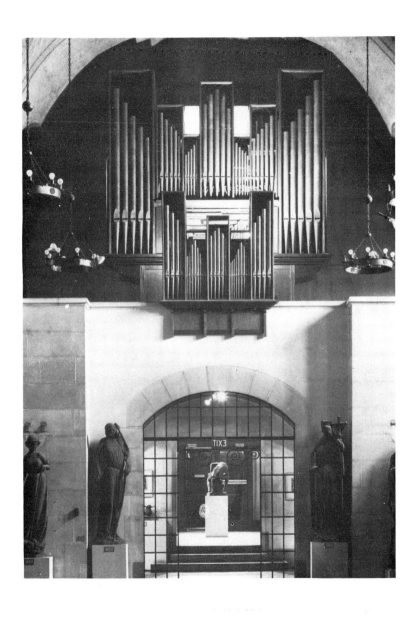

19. Busch-Reisinger Museum, Harvard University: Flentrop Organ.

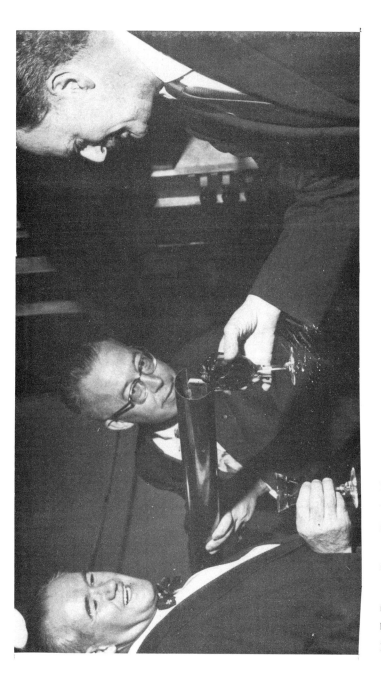

20. E. Power Biggs, D. A. Flentrop, and Charles Kuhn.

21. Music Hall, Methuen, Massachusetts: Walcker—Aeolian-Skinner Organ.

22. First Universalist Society, Newburyport, Massachusetts: Andover Organ.

23. Christ Church, Boston: Schlicker (Hutchings?) Organ.

24. Mount Calvary Church, Baltimore: Workmen from the original Andover Organ Co. installing the organ.

25. Mount Calvary Church: the keydesk.

is perhaps the first thorough, really great work of art . . . which we have yet had in this country," and the *Boston Daily Journal* called it ". . . the noblest instrument in the world and of all time."[49] The instrument was removed and stored in 1884 and was purchased by Edward F. Searles in 1897.

Searles built the now famous Methuen Music Hall especially for the organ. The reconstructed instrument was publicly heard again in 1909.[50] Although it thereafter gradually fell into disuse, its influence continued to be felt (especially by students in the New England area) and was renewed with the 1947 rebuilding, since which time the Music Hall has become a center for enthusiasts and lovers of organ music. This rebuild, like the instruments of Harrison and Holtkamp, was an electric action organ — in some ways quite out of the classic tradition — but it was a large step in the right direction.

About the Institute and the rebuilt organ, Howes comments:[51]

The Organ Institute was originally begun as an activity of the Methuen Memorial Music Hall, Incorporated. I was a member of its board, and, in fact, had been the instigator of the fund-raising which led to the purchase of the hall and the rebuilding of the organ. The hall and its contents, together with the organ factory which used to adjoin it, had been heavily mortgaged (by Ernest M. Skinner), so that the bank in Lawrence, Massachusetts took possession of the premises and, at the end of World War II, threatened to sell the building for industrial use. The bank officers sought me out . . . and it was not too difficult for me to enlist the interest and help of others in saving the hall and the instrument.

The rebuilt instrument was first heard in a recital in the spring of 1947,[52] in which Carl Weinrich, Ernest White, and I participated, we having all three acted as a committee of consultants for the rebuilding of the organ . . .

During Mr. Skinner's brief ownership and occupancy of the hall, he had occasion to remove the lowest octave of pipes from a number of stops in order to melt them down for pipe

---

[49]From "The Great Organ in the Boston Music Hall," Boston: Ticknor & Fields, 1865.

[50]From Arthur Howes, "The Methuen Organ," *Organ Institute Quarterly,* Andover, Mass.; Summer, 1951, p. 7.

[51]From correspondence with Arthur Howes, April 15, 1974.

[52]The impact of this event is almost comparable to the original hearings of the organ in 1863. The writer can testify to this, being then a wide-eyed student who sat in that audience.

*metal. He also sold at least one set of pipes outright and, in
general, made little attempt to keep the organ in good condition.
It was during this period, however, that the organ was used for
"pop" concerts.*

*. . . The organ was far too large for the building and,
from the very beginning, had many duplications . . . The committee decided to eliminate some of these and also not to replace
some of the stops that were wholly or partly missing. Since the
establishment of the organ in Methuen in the year just prior
to 1909 when it was first played there, it had included such
changes as increasing the scale of the Hauptwerk Principals by
three (or four?) pipes, new huge basses being added, and other
alterations had occurred which made some new pipe work absolutely necessary. We decided to ask for new Principals at 8',
4', 2 ⅔', and 2' pitch and to have the Mixtures reformed, as
the organ had been unwieldy. The most prominent Mixture on
the Great Organ had a conspicuous octave break at the 37th
note. Also, the Mixtures were full of gaps and holes, as for
instance, nothing between 4' and 1 ⅗' in some of them and the
Cornet of the Main work was a 16' Mixture and hence of
less use than it might have been. All of these things were
changed, and new Mixtures were provided for the Positiv, the
Swell, and the Choir, as well as Kleinmixture for the Great . . . .*

As Howes points out, the organ was too large for its home. It
was, in fact, too large to be an optimum instrument. With a Great
division of 21 stops, including three 16' registers and a Pedal division
of no less than 22 stops, including seven 16' registers and two 32'
registers, this instrument reflects the mania for bigness which was
already beginning in the nineteenth century when it was built, and
which continued with the rebuilding of 1909. (The 1863 *Great* had
23 complete registers; the *Pedal*, 20). Even in a very large hall, an
instrument of these proportions becomes redundant and unwieldy.
Such enormous organs are not so much "complete" as unnecessarily
eclectic; an instrument of half the size would probably play the
traditional repertoire better, because it would be possible for the
player to control it better and because chorus sound would blend
more cohesively on smaller windchests within a proper case.

Fulbright Scholars and Others in Europe, 1950-1960

At the same time that the Methuen Music Hall organ was gaining renewed influence, American teachers and students were trav-
elling in increasing numbers to play and learn from both old and

METHUEN, MASSACHUSETTS, MUSIC HALL[53]
As rebuilt by Donald Harrison, Aeolian-Skinner Organ Co., 1947

Great

- 16′ Principal
- 16′ Viola Major
- 16′ Bourdon
- 8′ Principal
- 8′ Gemshorn
- 8′ Gedeckt
- 5 ⅓′ Quint
- 4′ Octave
- 4′ Spitzflöte
- 4′ Koppelflöte
- 4′ Flûte d'Amour
- 3 ⅕′ Terz
- 2 ⅔′ Quint
- 2′ Super Octave
- 2′ Waldflöte
- 1 ⅗′ Terz
- 1 ⅐′ Septième
- Cornet VI
- Fourniture IV
- Scharf IV
- Kleine Mixtur IV

Choir

- 16′ Quintaten
- 8′ Viola
- 8′ Unda Maris
- 8′ Konzert Flöte
- 4′ Traversflöte
- 2′ Gemshorn
- Cymbel III
- 16′ Dulzian
- 8′ Krummhorn
- 4′ Regal

Positiv

- 8′ Gedeckt
- 8′ Quintaten
- 4′ Principal
- 4′ Nachthorn
- 2 ⅔′ Nasat
- 2′ Oktav
- 2′ Blockflöte
- 1 ⅗′ Terz
- 1 ⅓′ Quinta
- 1′ Super Oktav
- Scharf III
- Zimbel III

Swell

- 8′ Principal
- 8′ Viole-de-Gambe
- 8′ Viole Celeste
- 8′ Flûte à Cheminée
- 8′ Aeoline
- 4′ Prestant
- 4′ Flûte Couverte
- 2 ⅔′ Nazard
- 2′ Piccolo
- 2′ Octavin
- 1 ⅗′ Tierce
- Plein Jeu IV
- 16′ Basson
- 8′ Trompette
- 8′ Hautbois
- 4′ Clairon

(*Continued on next page*)

---

[53]From Arthur Howes, "The Methuen Organ," *Organ Institute Quarterly,* Andover, Mass.; Summer, 1951.

(Continued from previous page)

Pedal

32′	Principal	4′	Nachthorn
16′	Principal	3 ⅕′	Terz
16′	Contre Basse	2′	Waldflöte
16′	Bourdon		Grand Bourdon IV
16′	Quintade		Mixtur VI
16′	Lieblich Gedeckt	32′	Contre Bombarde
8′	Octave	16′	Bombarde
8′	Cello	16′	Bassoon
8′	Spitzflöte	8′	Trompette
5 ⅓′	Quint	4′	Clairon
4′	Super Octave	2′	Rohr Schalmei

modern instruments in Europe. When the writer spent a student summer in Europe in 1951, Fenner Douglass had already been in France, Holland, and Germany investigating organs, and was beginning to influence students through his teaching at the Oberlin Conservatory. Robert Noehren, having been in Europe in the late '40's, inspired his own students at the University of Michigan to go and see for themselves. In 1956 E. Power Biggs was introduced to the Schnitger organ at Zwolle, which had just been restored by D. A. Flentrop. Hugh Porter, Dean of the Union Seminary School of Music, visited Zwolle that same year and in 1957 Frank Bozyan of the Yale School of Music made the same pilgrimage. By this time the remarkable opportunities offered by the Fulbright Program had enabled significant numbers of other music students to learn from European instruments. Arthur Howes' European organ tours beginning in the late '50's also enabled many to see and hear for the first time. The cumulative influence of these teachers and players on American builders was telling, not least because they often proceeded to import instruments for their institutions from the best European makers when few if any mechanical action organs were being made in this country. American makers had to pay attention, even if they did not wish to; luckily several were already excited by what they were learning from Europe.

Imported Organs in the '50's: Music Schools, Churches, but not Seminaries

During the 1950's an impressive group of music schools began to install mechanical action instruments for practice, teaching, or public use. Students were able to observe at first hand the differences between these organs and those with electric actions and different tonal design. The end result has been a consistently growing demand for tracker organs.

It is noteworthy that imported instruments appeared in small institutions (often where new young teachers had been in Europe or been influenced by such men as Noehren or Douglass) as well as in larger, well-known schools.

Robert Noehren had a Rieger mechanical action studio organ at the University of Michigan by 1952; Oberlin Conservatory got a Flentrop Positiv in 1956; Salem College in North Carolina had a Flentrop instrument in 1957; Alabama College had a Flentrop in 1960; the Yale School of Music Flentrop studio organs arrived in 1962; the New England Conservatory's studio instrument by Metzler came in 1961, and in 1958 Oberlin got its second Flentrop instrument (which had been used to test acoustics at the Busch-Rei-

singer Museum before completion of the present organ there). The
first large imported instrument for a church was Beckerath's organ
for Trinity Lutheran Church, Cleveland, in 1957; the first sizable
University organ, also by Beckerath, was at Stetson University,
Deland, Florida, in 1961. The instrument by Noel Mander at the
Churchill Memorial in Fulton, Missouri; large Flentrop instruments
in Seattle's St. Mark's Cathedral (1965) and at Oberlin Conservatory (1974); The State University of New York at Purchase; and
the Frobenius organ in the Congregational Church, Cambridge,
indicate that importing did not end with the entry of American
makers into the mechanical action market.

Although music schools and some churches were waking up to
the influx of imaginative ideas coming from abroad and the beginning experiments in the United States, a disappointing lack of
interest characterized seminary chapels. Several electric action organs
of advanced design appeared in some seminaries, as already noted,
but already relatively late in the game. Considering the immense
influence that the musical training (or the lack of it) of the clergy
has on what sort of instrument will appear in churches, this in-
difference in the seminaries represented the loss of a major frontier.
That not one major seminary had a classic mechanical action organ
by 1960 is disappointing; that the then-flourishing School of Sacred
Music at Union Seminary, New York, had managed to turn its
back on the new artistic state of affairs, rather than being in the
vanguard, is almost incredible.

Also to be mentioned is the 19-stop instrument by Otto Hoffman
(1956), for which Flentrop supplied the pipes, with a case designed
by Joseph Blanton after the Flentrop case in Groenlo, The Netherlands. This instrument, in the Matthews Memorial Presbyterian
Church at Albany, Texas, and the 1954 Flentrop Positiv in the University Presbyterian Church, San Antonio, are probably the first
encased mechanical action organs to appear in the United States.
The Albany case was not partitioned for each division of the organ,
but it was related in scale to the size of the instrument. Although
unencased, the first Rieger "portable" organs, especially the one in
the Rogers Auditorium of the Metropolitan Museum (c. 1952),
exerted considerable influence.

Rebuilding American Mechanical Action Organs

Organists and organ builders, reacting to the combined influences
of European travels, imported instruments, and the growing interest
in the repertoire of the seventeenth and eighteenth centuries, began

to think more about saving existing mechanical action organs in the
U. S. and less about electrifying or destroying them. Since almost
no instruments from the eighteenth century remained, the candi-
dates for reconstruction were usually nineteenth-century organs,
often with unwieldy dispositions, actions, and scalings. Because of
the initial dominance of North European tonal ideas (as distin-
guished from French or other styles), attempts were made to turn
nineteenth-century American tracker organs into more or less Schnit-
ger-style instruments, with some concessions to English or French
ideas. In some instances the instrument chosen presented formidable
difficulties, and in others, the builder's lack of experience with
mechanical action or voicing on low-pressure with slider chests made
for less than ideal results. Nonetheless, these efforts represented another step in the right direction and the lessons learned from such
projects could be applied to later ones. Three examples, each involving a highly-motivated organist in collaboration with a maker,
come to mind:

In 1950 the large Johnson organ of 1893 in Grace Church,
Sandusky, Ohio, was rebuilt by Herman Schlicker in collaboration
with Robert Noehren, whose experience in Europe in the late '40's
had spurred his interest in organ design as well as in organ playing. Noehren proceeded to record on this instrument, of which the
jacket notes say the following:[54]

> . . . This work was done under the direction of Robert
> Noehren, who planned a new disposition and specified the
> scales and voicing details of the pipework . . . Of unique in-
> terest is the retention of the mechanical action which was a part
> of the old organ . . . The voicing of this organ is quite unlike
> that of modern organs . . . It reflects the serious studies Robert
> Noehren has made of certain old organs in Holland and Ger-
> many . . . His studies have concentrated upon an attempt to
> consider more seriously the relation of organ building to the
> playing of organ music, and he believes the art of organ build-
> ing must be closely related to musical taste . . . The organ of
> Grace Church in Sandusky, Ohio, represents the first serious
> attempt in America to combine the use of mechanical action and
> certain traditional principles of voicing.

In 1957 the church authorities of the First Universalist Society
of Newburyport, Massachusetts, were about to electrify or replace
the organ made in 1834 by Joseph Alley (and modified by Hutch-

---

[54] Jacket notes for Allegro Recording AL 116 (Robert Noehren playing the
Sandusky organ: Bach, *Canonic Variations* and *Partita*, "O Gott du
frommer Gott").

ings in 1889). They sought the advice of Melville Smith, who recommended that the organ not be discarded but be rebuilt by Charles Fisk, who had recently acquired the Andover Organ Company nearby. The mechanical action was retained, except for the addition of an electric action Pedal, and the original pipes were incorporated into the rebuilt instrument in its handsome original case.

In 1958, E. Power Biggs' advice resulted in the reconstruction by Herman Schlicker of the nineteenth-century organ by Hutchings (or Simmons?) in the eighteenth-century case (by Thomas Johnston, enlarged by Goodrich in the 1830's) in Christ Church (the "Old North" Church) in Boston. Again, an electric action Pedal was added, and most pipes were new, but the nineteenth-century mechanical action was retained. In this instance, all problems with the action were not solved and the myth that the organ itself is from the eighteenth century still occasionally surfaces, but again, this was a step in the right direction.

IV

BALTIMORE 1961: TURNING POINT IN AMERICAN ORGAN DESIGN

The Breakthrough

The organ created in 1961 by Charles Fisk and his associates. for Mount Calvary Church, Baltimore, is the first sizable mechanical-action organ built in the U. S. in this century. Its musical and historical importance, more visible now after the passage of substantial time, can hardly be overemphasized. It is the first instrument in classical European style and American rendering in which all of the destructive compromises previously countenanced were avoided. The artistic objective was, as Fisk has put it, "That old music be played right." Therefore, no critical concessions to twentieth-century American practices were allowed, because the relation between the instrument and the repertoire it was to play was paramount.

The Baltimore organ reflects the growing influences from Europe, which were more and more strongly felt here after 1945 because of or owing to student pilgrimages to Europe, the importation of European organs, recordings made on early instruments, and' the general heightening of interest in music written before 1750. In the design and construction of the Baltimore organ each of the classic essentials for an optimum design was treated as it might have been in the early eighteenth century:

1. The *Disposition* consists of three divisions, each containing a complete flue chorus with appropriate reeds at a variety of pitches.

2. The *wind supply* for each division is provided by a large reservoir at low wind pressure (1¾" for manuals, 2⅜" for Pedal).

3. The *Voicing* and *Scaling* take into account the relationship of each register to the rest of the division, as well as to the acous-

tical properties of the case and the building. Due attention is given
to balancing the width of the windway and the foot hole of the
pipe. Classic voicing techniques employ a minimum of nicking.

4. *Cases*, shallow, with thin walls, serve to project and blend
the sound and to give identity to each division. The case design is a
synthesis of cases at Amiens, Dortmund and Sion.

5. *Placement*, against the west wall and relatively high in the
building, allows the sound to flow unobstructed down the length
of the church.

6. The *Acoustics* of the building, the result of a large volume
of space enclosed by reflective, natural structural materials, enhance
the organ sound.

7. The *Action* (slider chests with carefully balanced mechanical
key and stop action) provides unanimity of speech from the pipes
and rhythmic control for the player. The Hoofdwerk employs *traction suspendre*. In *traction (mechanique) suspendre* the weight of
the action hangs from the pallets instead of resting on the keys.
This results in a lighter and more even action.

Earlier and more modest attempts in designing mechanical-action
organs had been made in the United States, including several by
Fisk and associates in the old Andover Company. In general these
were either on too small a scale to attract wide notice, or they
amounted to the rebuilding of nineteenth-century organs. In some
instances, builders were still too inexperienced to produce both a
work of art and a functioning instrument.

Now that considerable time has passed, the originality and signifi-
cance of the Baltimore organ can be appreciated by comparing the
totality of that solution to the partial solutions which were usual
for the time. Perhaps the main fallacy in earlier American attempts
to make "European style" instruments was the naive hope that there
was some single secret, some mysterious trick or forgotten technique,
which would produce an optimum design. Many of the important
principles had already been rediscovered by electric action builders,
but always without a clear understanding of their relative importance
in the context of all the principles essential to classic organ-building.

First among these principles came adherence to the classic disposition. Perhaps the next important basic idea to come from a
knowledge of European organs was that good sound was influenced
by location: putting organ pipes in a room separate from the listener
obstructed the production of clear, lively sounds. This point was
doggedly made by Walter H. Holtkamp, who in most instances even
discarded the case. Then followed a number of ideas: that the use
of slider chests, or voicing with open footholes and no nicking, or

light wind pressure, or copying scales from early organs, would accomplish the miracle. These were all improvements, but the miracle still did not happen, because only part of the problem was understood, and only a partial remedy could be imagined.

What was needed was a coherent concept of what an organ is — or should be — and what factors give it form and limitations, and therefore identity. This approach required not only technical, musical, and historical knowledge, but also considerable humility, to enable the builder to understand why earlier organs worked and sounded well. He had to avoid viewing old organs only through the eyes of the modern technologist, convinced that the "old" ways of doing things must always be improved upon, else they will be inadequate to meet modern requirements.

With the organ, as with the harpsichord, it develops that the requisite musical and technical skills were brought to a very high degree of perfection several hundred years ago. Builders and players alike had been seduced and misled by the idea that an instrument must be "modern" to make sense, without stopping to think that they could not and did not wish to apply the same unthinking requirement to the music which was written for these instruments. So it has become clear, at last, that not one, but all of the characteristics common to the instruments admired in Europe are essential to our making them ourselves. It has also developed that a proper acoustical environment is essential, and that the organ must be understood as part of the architecture and carefully related to the space in which it is placed.

It was the new assimilation of the old truths which made the design of the Baltimore instrument possible. To keep its identity and fulfill its musical purposes, an organ must have a proper disposition related to the space in which it sounds; a proper chest and key action; wind supply; voicing and regulation; a case; a good acoustical environment; and a direct, mechanical linkage between the player and the instrument. The Baltimore organ may signal the end of a long and arduous search in which many thoughtful men have joined; more importantly, it marks the beginning of a surer and more artistic approach to organ building in this country.

Yankee Ingenuity and European Antecedents

The style of André and Jean André Silbermann more than any other probably influenced the Baltimore design. This is borne out most by the quality of the voicing; also by the number of *tierces*, as well as the style of the reeds, particularly on the manual divisions.

Except for the 8′ reed, the Pedal division is more closely related to the North European ideal of an extensive pallette of pitches and tone colors, perhaps most specifically the work of the Schnitger family. The *Great Trumpet,* mounted *en chamade,* is derived from Iberian practice, which has affected modern European builders as well as Americans — an international, if somewhat isolated stylistic influence.[55]

The disposition of the Baltimore organ can be best understood with reference to the kinds of instruments which were its antecedents. More or less typical organs by Arp Schnitger (Steinkirchen, 1687) and Andreas Silbermann (Arlesheim, 1761) have been selected to make this point (see p. 28 and p. 29). Both are encased, although as noted above, the Pedal division of the Silbermann is placed in the open behind the main case. Originally this was at least partly due to different requirements in the repertoire: the demands made by eighteenth-century French composers for an independent pedal were considerably fewer than those made by the Germans, whose music regularly required an independent Pedal division, capable of carrying either a *cantus* in any of several registers or a polyphonic line equal to those played on the manuals.

The Builders of the Baltimore Organ

The chance to build an organ of 36 stops came somewhat unexpectedly to the small firm of Andover. The church (where Arthur Howes, the organist, was the driving force to acquire a classic instrument) had initially considered the firms of Frobenius and Marcussen in Denmark and Flentrop in Holland, all of whom had long delivery times. D. A. Flentrop, who served as a consultant for the organ, recommended Fisk; Howes and MacAllister Ellis, Rector of Mount Calvary, agreed.

When the organ for Mount Calvary Church was built, Charles Fisk was President of the Andover Organ Company. His colleagues who made substantial contributions to this instrument were Leo Constantineau, Fritz Noack, and Walter Hawkes. Shortly after the completion of this instrument, Fisk moved the physical and corporate belongings of the original company from Methuen to Gloucester, Massachusetts, relinquishing the old corporate name to Constantineau and Robert Reich, who set up a new business in Methuen in the old Andover workshop. They became the present Andover Organ Company, and Fisk became known as C. B. Fisk, Inc., located in Gloucester. Hawkes presently went to work for Fritz Noack, who

---

[55]cf. Dispositions of Arlesheim & Steinkirchen on p. 28 & p. 29.

MOUNT CALVARY CHURCH, BALTIMORE (1961)

Manuals C − g′′′; Pedal C − g′

Hoofdwerk
- 16′ Bourdon
- 8′ Prestant
- 8′ Roerfluit
- 8′ Fluitdous
- 4′ Octaaf
- 4′ Spitsfluit
- 2 ⅔′ Quint
- 2′ Superoctaaf
- 2′ Blokfluit
- Mixtuur IV
- Cymbaal III
- Cornet III
- 8′ Trompet

Rugwerk
- 8′ Holpijp
- 8′ Quintadeen
- 4′ Prestant
- 4′ Roerpijp
- 2 ⅔′ Nasard
- 2′ Octaaf
- 1 ⅗′ Terts
- 1 ⅓′ Quinta
- 1′ Siffluit
- Scherp III
- 8′ Krumhoorn

Pedaal
- 16′ Subbas
- 16′ Lieflijk Gedekt
- 8′ Octaaf
- 8′ Gedektpommer
- 4′ Superoctaaf
- 4′ Vlakfluit
- 2′ Nachthoorn
- Ruispijp IV
- Mixtuur IV
- 16′ Fagot
- 8′ Trompet
- 4′ Schalmei

Couplers:
Rugwerk - Pedaal
Rugwerk - Hoofdwerk

Adjustable combination
Pedal, affecting *Pedaal*
and *Hoofdwerk.*

Zymbelstern

had gone out on his own a year earlier, but whose contribution to the Baltimore instrument was noteworthy. Hawkes later returned to Andover.

Fisk undertook the tonal and mechanical design, scaling and voicing, and the case design is jointly the work of Fisk and Constantineau. The carving is the handiwork of Constantineau.

The nameboard of the organ reads "Andover-Flentrop," although D. A. Flentrop, aside from supplying the turned grenadillo stop knobs, served as a consultant, and did not participate directly in the construction of the instrument. The keyboards, now with ebony naturals and ivory-capped sharps, were made in the shop of William Dowd. (The naturals were originally covered with cocobolo with ebony sharps. This was changed in 1968 by Dowd at Fisk's request.) The wooden pipes were made by the Andover Company. Metal pipes were imported from Rieger in Austria, Muhleisen in Strasbourg, and Jacques Stinkens in The Netherlands.

The Dutch terminology for stop names was at the request of Arthur Howes and reflects the wish to emphasize the connection of this instrument with European prototypes. The voluminous correspondence between Howes and the builders (on which much of the above is based) over a period of many months, testifies to the fastidious care which was lavished on every detail of this instrument by all concerned with its design and construction.

The pipes for the 8′ Trompet of the *Hoofdwerk* are placed *en chamade* in the front of the main case. Although this was part of the original design, the 13 bass pipes were initially mounted inside the case. Fisk moved them to their proper position in the case front in 1966.

Commenting on an early draft of this chapter, Charles Fisk had this to say about the Baltimore organ:

> *You've talked about the ways in which the Baltimore organ conforms to a (modern) European idea, but why is it art? After all, there are plenty of other organs which obey all the rules you've mentioned, but sound pretty ordinary . . . I think it's unusual because it came as a new idea to several people with imagination, who didn't really try to copy, but who took forms and ideas out of books and pictures and records, and strung them together in a way that meant something to them. Three months' voicing didn't hurt any . . . I wasn't trying to follow anybody else's rules, or if I was, I was thinking of them as my own rules. The organ is a typically American rehash of European notions — naive, non-academic — it's an example of a pro-*

cess that has gone on here ever since people came here from Europe.

V

POSTSCRIPT: STYLE AND ELECTICISM
IN ORGAN DESIGN

Although the music of Bach had been revered since its mid-nineteenth-century revival led by Mendelssohn, the problem of playing a diverse repertoire with appropriate sounds had not come up in the U. S. with much force until the 1940's. It was only after World War II that much of the repertoire itself became easily available. Until that time, nineteenth-century music and transcriptions pretty much ruled the day, a situation which quickly changed with the availability of good European editions of volume after volume of important music from the seventeenth and eighteenth centuries. Gradually, players became convinced that the style of the music itself was inherently bound up with the style of the instrument for which it was intended. Despite qualities common to the various "classic" styles, each was distinctive in some way, which made its native repertoire more successful than music from another time or place.

One partial design solution lay in using the instruments of one style period as models. This is all very well, in the case of Germanic instruments, for instance, if only the music of the high Baroque in North Europe is considered. But what about French, Spanish, English, or Italian repertoire of even the same era?

This was the problem that both Walter Holtkamp and Donald Harrison set out to solve. At their best, they were successful to an impressive degree. The Syracuse University instrument and that at the Church of the Advent, Boston, are two examples, still relatively unchanged, of how each approached the solution.

If, for simplicity, one deals only with the difference between the organs of France and North Europe in the early eighteenth century (to say nothing of nineteenth-century French music, which makes still different demands), the inherent frustrations are quickly evident: The often wide difference in Mixture pitches and the place of the reeds in ensemble (in Germany) or as a much more dominant quality (in France), are two examples of the differences encountered.

Another partial solution was simply to make the organ larger, to include, say, both a *Brust* and an *Echo/Recit,* as well as a *Great* and *Positiv,* and perhaps a nineteenth-century French or English *Swell* as well. This turned out to be not only expensive and unwieldy, but also to invite an eclectic design made up of parts which may not make sense as a whole. For instance, Harrison's organ for St. Paul's Chapel, Columbia University, had five divisions (Great, Swell, Choir, Positiv, Brustwerke [sic], plus Pedal, for a total of 61 independent registers plus four Pedal borrows). Both Holtkamp and Harrison might well have been more nearly successful, had they been subject to the limitations imposed on mechanical-action makers, who are less bewitched by the idea that one instrument must play absolutely all the repertoire. It is better that the designer make some judgments about the segments of the repertoire for which an instrument is primarily intended, and do his best to allow for musical, if not "authentic," performance of other music. Since the bulk of the repertoire falls between 1650 and 1750, the direction of the basic design is clear.

Another partial solution was to lavish special concern on voicing and scaling of the pipework. Although this was important to both Holtkamp and Harrison, it is fair to say that the voicing appropriate to slider chests and the resulting pipe speech were not logically obtainable with electro-pneumatic chests. Also, the voicing techniques used for electric action did not work well with slider chests, although Holtkamp often used slider chests, at least for the *Great* division.

There are no all-purpose instruments offering easy solutions, but intelligent mating of the repertoire and the instrument can produce an organ of reasonable versatility, which still has an identity of its own. For example, an instrument on which the *Passacaglia in c minor* and the *Canonic Variations* of Bach, as well as the organ masses of Couperin can be musically performed, need not be of staggering size. Yet in these works the main requirements of all the music of France and North Europe between 1650 and 1750 are included.

It is certainly true that Spanish, Italian, and English music make some important demands for unique sounds (the fiery horizontal reed registers and the brilliant *Cornetas* in Spanish instruments, the *Voce Umana* in Italian instruments). Fortunately, these requirements can be musically if not authentically met in an instrument which will perform the more extensive French and North European repertoire. The basic requirements for accompanying congregational singing are sufficiently straightforward that they are inevitably met by a well-placed and well-designed instrument in any of several styles. The modern problem is that of designing an instrument which has a clear identity in the sense that all classic organs do and which is not irrevocably limited to only one style of repertoire.

To be both artistic and realistic, a proposal for a design can be made only for a specific situation and place, and it should be made by the organ-builder, not the musician, however important his advice might be to the builder. Therefore, the temptation to close this chapter with dispositions for instruments of varying sizes has been resisted on the advice of organ-builders. It is in order nonetheless to outline the resources that an optimum instrument, even of modest size (say 20 registers) must contain, if it is to play the repertoire adequately.

Very generally, the repertoire is characterized by:

1. The use of antiphonal effects between two or even three divisions.
2. The use of polyphonic textures, which demands several separate voices of equal clarity.
3. The use of "solo and accompaniment", requiring a variety of both reed and flue sounds, the latter at a variety of pitches or with combined pitches (as in the Cornet).

The basic tonal resources can be summarized as follows:

1. A chorus sound consisting of at least 8', 4', 2', Mixture on each of two keyboards plus a comparable Pedal chorus, for *forte* polyphonic or chordal effects (including support of congregational singing). For the *Grand Jeu*, required in much French music, an 8' Trumpet, a 16' Bourdon, and a *Tierce* are mandatory in the *Great*, as well as an 8' Trumpet in the Pedal.
2. As many combinations for the playing of Trios on two keyboards and uncoupled Pedal as possible: for instance 8' and 2' versus 8' and 4' and 1 ⅓', against 8' and 4' in the bass (or an 8' reed register versus flues 8' and 4', etc.) For French music, a *Cornet* versus an 8' *Cromorne* is mandatory, with an 8' bass in the Pedal.
3. A variety of reed and flue sounds, appropriate for playing plain or ornamented solo lines on keyboards and in

the Pedal. For North European chorale *cantus* playing, a 4′ stop is necessary in the Pedal, as is an 8′ Trumpet for French plainsong *cantus* lines.

4. An adjustable *Tremulant* is desirable for much of the repertoire and is essential for some French music.

As concluding cautions, it must be remembered that success depends on placement and acoustical environment as well as the disposition, encasement, action, and voicing; and, finally, that undue concern for "versatility" can destroy the concept of the instrument, either by blurring the basic principles of design or by causing the instrument to reach unmanageable proportions.

TERMINOLOGY

Pitch and Keyboard Ranges

Keyboard ranges are given in terms of the standard designations based on the position of a note on the keyboard. Thus, middle c is written c′, tenor c as lower case c, Great C as C, and Contra-C as CC. The low C on Pedal or manual is shown as C, regardless of the sounding pitch of sub-unison registers. The tendency to show the low C of the Pedal as CC or even CCC, since the division might be based on 16′ pitch, is confusing and has therefore been avoided.

Stop names, spelling, and pipe shapes

The precision originally observed in naming registers in each of the European styles unfortunately no longer obtains. American builders have long made a polyglot use, characteristic of our eclectic language, of English, French, German, Spanish, and Italian terms. A register labeled "Stopt Diapason" by John Snetzler or "Gedeckt" by Arp Schnitger might sound quite different from one similarly labeled by an American maker.

There are wide differences in specific sound of pipes answering to the same name. There is occasional discrepancy between what the builder calls the register on the stop knob and the shape of the pipes, or in the case of reed stops, whether they are full, half, or quarter length. The player must first of all use his ears, but he must also understand how all the elements of pipe construction and voicing affect both speech and timbre, if he is to register appropriately.

Predictably, the Germans were more consistent than others in naming stops. Although it may be useful to anglicize terms, it is important to re-establish the regard for relation between the shape or length of the pipe itself, whether it is fully open or stopped, etc., and its sound. More than a summary of terms would run to many pages, since some makers have experimented endlessly with pipe shapes, especially reed resonators and canister configurations. Also, either wood or metal has been used, without drastic effect on the sound, to construct many registers. However, the following terms, particularly in North Europe, connote shape and length, and in the case of mixtures, pitch, as shown:

Flues

Gedeckt, Stopped Diapason	cylindrical, stopped
Gemshorn	tapered, narrow scale
Koppelflute	cylindrical with tapered canister, half opened at top
Nachthorn	cylindrical, wide scale
Principal (Montre, Diapason)	cylindrical, open; "Prestant" is often used for the Principal rank of basic pitch which is displayed in the case of each division
Rohrflute	cylindrical, chimney piercing canister
Spitzflute	tapered, wide scale

Reeds

Cromorne, Krummhorn	half-length, cylindrical, covered
Dulzian	half-length or quarter-length, cylindrical, covered
Fagot, Bassoon	half-length, conical, covered
Hautbois, Oboe	half- or full-length, with double cone
Posaune, Bazuin, Bombarde, Trombone	full-length, conical, open
Rankett	resonators often of more or less equal length, usually wood, covered, with perforations near bottom
Regal	cylindrical or conical, sometimes with canisters of varying shapes

Schalmei	half-length, cylindrical, covered
Trompette, Clarion	full-length, conical, open
Vox Humana	quarter-length, cylindrical, covered

Usual Mixture pitches at C

Cimbel — $\frac{1}{3}'$ (repeating every 12 notes)
Fourniture — $2'$ or $1\frac{1}{3}'*$
Mixture — $1\frac{1}{3}'$
Rauschquint — $2\frac{2}{3}'$
Scharff — $\frac{2}{3}'$
Cimbala — $\frac{1}{2}'$
Lleno — $1\frac{1}{3}'$

---

*According to Dom Bédos, depending whether on *Grand Orgue* or *Positiv*. By the same token, Cymbale would be either $1'$ or $\frac{1}{2}'$ depending on location.

SOURCES CITED IN TEXT AND SELECTED REFERENCES

It is difficult to suggest works useful to the interested reader with limited technical information. As a start, a brief list, consisting of general works on organ building and especially pertinent articles (available and in English), is indicated by asterisks.

Adlung, M. Jacob, *Musica Mechanica Organoedi*, Berlin: 1768 (Facsimile, Kassel: 1931, Barenreiter).

De Amezua, Ramon Gonzalez, *Perspectivas para la Historia del Organo Espanol*, Madrid: 1970, Real Academia de Bellas Artes de San Fernando.

*Anderson, Poul-Gerhard, tr. Joanne Curnutt, *Organ Building and Design*, London: 1969, George Allen and Unwin Ltd.

Anon., *The Great Organ in the Boston Music Hall*, Boston: 1865, Ticknor and Fields.

Antegnati, C., *L'Arte Organica*, Brescia: 1608 (Reprint, Mainz: 1958, Rheingold).

Barnes, William H., *The Contemporary American Organ*, 3rd (and later) edition, New York: 1937, J. Fischer & Bro.

Bédos de Celles, Dom François, *L'Art du Facteur d'Orgues*, Paris: 1766: reprint Kassel: 1965, Barenreiter. (An English translation is in preparation by the Sunbury Press.)

Le Begue, Nicolas, Preface to *Premier Livre d'Orgue*, Paris: 1676. (Reprint, Johnson Reprint Corporation, 1972: New York.)

*Beranek, Leo, *Music, Acoustics and Architecture*, New York: 1962, John Wiley and Sons, Inc.

*Blanton, Joseph, *The Organ in Church Design*, Albany, Texas: 1957, Venture Press.

*................., *The Revival of the Organ Case*, Albany, Texas: 1965, Venture Press.

Blodgett, Walter, Notes for Inaugural Concert, McMyler Memorial Organ, Cleveland Museum of Art, Cleveland: 1971.

Brunzema, Daniel, *Die Gestaltung des Orgelprospektes im Friesischen und Angrenzenden Nordseeküstengebiet* . . . . Norden: 1958,Verlag Ostfriesische Landschaft Aurich.

*Clutton, C. and Niland, A., *The British Organ*, London, 1963, Batsford.

Collins, George, "Transfer of Thin Tile Masonry from Spain to the U. S.," *Journal of the Society of Architectural Historians*.

Davison, Archibald T., *Church Music*, Cambridge: 1952, Harvard Press.

................., *Protestant Church Music in America*, Boston: 1933, E. C. Schirmer.

*Douglass, Fenner, *The Language of the Classical French Organ*, New Haven: 1967, Yale University Press.

Ellinwood, L., *History of American Church Music*, New York: 1953, Morehouse-Gorham.

Enrico, Eugene, *The Orchestra at San Petronio in the Baroque Era*, Washington: in press, Smithsonian Institution Press.

Farnam, Lynnwood, "Lynnwood Farnam Tells of Recent Trip in Europe", two articles, *The Diapason*, Nov. 1, 1923 and January 1, 1924.

Fesperman, J., *A Snetzler Chamber Organ of 1761*, Washington: 1970, Smithsonian Institution Press.

*Fesperman, J. and Hinshaw, D., "New Light on North America's Oldest Instruments: Mexico", *Organ Yearbook*, 1972.

*Fisk, C. B., "The Organ's Breath of Life", *The Diapason*, September, 1963.

*...................................., (with Edward W. Flint, John Ferris and Barbara J. Owen) "Organ", article in *Harvard Dictionary of Music*, 2nd edition, Cambridge: 1969, Belknap Press.

Flentrop, Dirk A., *tr.* J. Fesperman, "Restoration of the Zwolle Organ", *Organ Institute Quarterly*, VII:2 (Summer 1957).

Flint, Edward W., "American Organ Building after the War" (Oct., 1944), *MS* Smithsonian Institution (Submitted to *The Organ*, Oct. 23, 1944, but not published, probably due to destruction by bombing in London.)

...................................., *The Newberry Memorial Organ at Yale University*, New Haven: 1930, Yale University Press.

Hess, J., *Dispositien der Merkwaardigste Kerk-Orgelen*, Gouda: 1774 (Reprint, J. A. H. Wagenaar, Utrecht: 1945).

Holtkamp, W. H., *Present Day Trends in Organ Building*, Cleveland: 1940, published by the author.

Howes, Arthur, "The Methuen Organ", *Organ Institute Quarterly*, Summer, 1951.

Hinshaw, David, "Four Centuries of Mexican Organs", *Music*, May, June, 1969.

*Hubbard, Frank, *Three Centuries of Harpsichord Making*, Cambridge: 1965, Harvard University Press.

Kobel, Heinz, "Die Orgel des Johann Andreas Silbermann von 1761 im Dom zu Arlesheim . . .", *Katholische Kirchenmusik*, Vol. 2, 1962, Schwyz: E. Eberhard.

Lindley, Mark, "Mersenne on Keyboard Tuning", *MS*, Smithsonian Institution.

...................................., "The Clavier Diversely Tempered", *MS*, Smithsonian Institution.

Matthews, Betty, *Index to THE ORGAN*, Bournemouth: 1970, Kenneth Mummery Ltd.

Mendel, A., "On Pitches in Use in Bach's Time", *Musical Quarterly*, XLI:332 ff and 466 ff.

Morris, Danny, "City Hall Station", 1972: *MS*, Smithsonian Institution; Paper delivered at first Annual Conference, Society for Industrial Archeology (*in re* Guastavino tiles).

Nye, Eugene M., "Walter Holtkamp — A Master Organ Builder", *The Organ*, No. 202: Vol. II, Oct. 1971.

*Ochse, Orpha, *The History of the Organ in the United States*, Bloomington: 1975, University of Indiana Press.

*Peeters, F. and Vente, M., *The Organ and Its Music*. Antwerp, 1971. Mercatorfonds.

Poister, A., Paper on Holtkamp Organ, Syracuse University. See Wells, Lester.

Powell, Newman W., *Early Keyboard Fingering and Its Effect on Articulation*, *MS*, Department of Music, Stanford University, 1954.

Rizzo, Jeanne, "Lynwood Farnam — Master Organist of the Century", *The Diapason*, December, 1974.

Routley, Erik, *Church Music and Theology*, Philadelphia: 1959, Muhlenberg Press.

Thomas, W. R. and Rhodes, J. J. K., "Schlick, Praetorius and the History of Organ Pitch", *Organ Yearbook*, 1971.

Vennum, Thomas, "The Registration of Frescobaldi's Organ Music", *Organ Institute Quarterly*, XI: 1 & 2, 1964.

Wells, Lester G., "Some Historical Notes on Pipe Organs at Syracuse University", Syracuse: 1954, Syracuse University Library, including paper read by Arthur Poister for American Guild of Organists, April 16, 1961, at Crouse Auditorium, Syracuse University.

*Williams, Peter, *The European Organ*, London: 1966, Batsford.

*Wilson, Michael, *The English Chamber Organ*, Columbia: 1968, University of South Carolina Press.

Wyly, James, "La Registrazione della Musica Organistica dei Francesco Correa de Arauxo", *L'Organo*, Anno. VIII, N. 1 (English summary).

........................., *The Pre-Romantic Spanish Organ: Its Structure, Literature and Use in Performance*, Ann Arbor: 1967, University Microfilms, Inc.

INDEX

Many *concepts* not found in this index of *names* can easily be located in the table of contents printed in the front of the book.